Cases in Technological Entrepreneurship

Converting Ideas into Value

Edited by

Claudio Petti

Assistant Professor, Scuola Superiore ISUFI/e-Business Management Section, University of Salento, Italy

Preface by

Aldo Romano

Director of the Scuola Superiore ISUFI University of Salento, Italy

Edward Elgar

Cheltenham, UK • Northampton, MA, USA

Published by
Edward Elgar Publishing Limited
The Lypiatts
15 Lansdown Road
Cheltenham
Glos GL50 2JA
UK

Edward Elgar Publishing, Inc.
William Pratt House
9 Dewey Court
Northampton
Massachusetts 01060
USA

A catalogue record for this book
is available from the British Library

Library of Congress Control Number: 2009921533

Mixed Sources
Product group from well-managed
forests and other controlled sources
www.fsc.org Cert no. SA-COC-1565
© 1996 Forest Stewardship Council

FSC

ISBN 978 1 84844 186 6

Printed and bound by MPG Books Group, UK

Contents

Figures and tables

FIGURES

TABLES

Contributors

Fabrizio Cobis, Manager of Italian Ministry for Education, University and Research, Italy.

Mark Harris, Director of Higher Education and Research, Europe, Middle East, Africa Region at Intel, Germany and Associated Professor for Technology Entrepreneurship and Innovation at the University St Kliment Ohridski of Sofia, Bulgaria, and at the University Politechnica, Bucharest, Romania. Harris is also expert for the Executive MBA course at the Technical University of Munich.

Willem Hulsink, Professor of Entrepreneurship at the Erasmus University Rotterdam and Wageningen University & Research Centre, The Netherlands; **Tom Elfring**, Professor of Strategy and Entrepreneurship at the Free University, Amsterdam, The Netherlands; and **Wouter Stam**, Professor of Strategy and Entrepreneurship at the Free University, Amsterdam, The Netherlands.

William Lazonick, Professor at the University of Massachusetts Lowell, USA.

Maurice Olivier, Affiliated Professor at HEC Management School, University of Liege, Belgium and Co-founder and General Partner of BAMS Angels Fund, Belgium.

Claudio Petti, Assistant Professor in Global Strategy at the Scuola Superiore ISUFI, University of Salento, Italy.

Aldo Romano, Full Professor of Innovation Management at the Faculty of Engineering, and Director of the Scuola Superiore ISUFI, University of Salento, Italy.

Roberto Siagri, President and CEO of Eurotech Group, Italy; **Andrea Barbaro**, Investor Relations Manager and Strategic Planning Analyst at Eurotech Group, Italy; and **Nicola Buttolo**, CEO of Carpe Diem Valuenet, Italy.

David Verrill, Executive Director, MIT Center for Digital Business, USA.

Anthony I. Wasserman, Professor of Software Management Practice and Executive Director of The Center for Open Source Investigation, Carnegie Mellon Silicon Valley, USA.

Preface

The modern socio-economic environment is constantly reshaped by the incessant introduction of new technologies and related innovations. Today's entrepreneurs are associated with the capability to identify the distinctive and disruptive potential of emerging technologies and connected business opportunities that others might not see. This capability is a necessary, though not singularly sufficient, element in setting up a successful technology-based venture, fostering economic growth and increasing social well-being.

In an environment characterized by fast and fierce competition, a successful technological venture must have a compelling value proposition capable of rapidly going to market, possibly with a proven and sustainable business model, as well as a set of formal and informal supporting institutions. These are usually the charge of managers and civil servants.

Technological entrepreneurship is instrumental here; the process connects technology development with business creation. Specifically, the process entails the recognition or creation of potential business value of new discoveries and technologies and then matching these with existing and/or potential market needs. The ultimate goal is, of course, the transformation of those opportunities in commercial products, services and ultimately new businesses.

Even when such opportunities, compelling value propositions, markets, business models and related capabilities exist, the process is too complex to be handled by individuals or companies, no matter how talented or powerful they are. Technology-based entrepreneurial initiatives are inextricably linked and affected by their environmental context. This context can be a specific set of local conditions, or a particular country or region, or even a mix of cultural, organizational and technological aspects that affect technological development and entrepreneurship.

Converting ideas into value thus involves the integration of concepts within entrepreneurship and management as well as the involvement of governments and communities. This requires a shift in conventional thinking, from conceptual and organizational dichotomies towards a more holistic or 'dual' approach that transcends artificial boundaries of disciplines and specializations. Technological entrepreneurship is more of an art than a science – like 'ingredients' and 'regional recipes' that can be clarified by looking at the experiences of real actors and empirical findings, which can then be compared, adapted and adopted to a new context.

This volume draws on topics related to discussions from the Advanced International Summer School on 'Perspectives in Technological Entrepreneurship' held 11–14 July 2007 in Ostuni by the e-Business Management Section at the Scuola Superiore ISUFI, University of Salento, Italy. It provides a collection of cases and empirical studies that shed light on components and dynamics of the process of transformation of new ideas into value, that is, the technological entrepreneurship process. Distinguished contributors from Europe and the USA, from academia, industry and the public sector, provide experiences and empirical findings that address some of the following fundamental questions related to technological entrepreneurship:

- What is the role of entrepreneurship and technological innovation for economic growth and social well-being?
- Who are the main actors involved in this process and how they can shape a favorable context for generating, exploiting and spreading the benefits of technological innovations?
- How can governments, universities, private investors and companies interact to generate new technologies that are able to be transformed into corporate and societal gains?
- What is the role of networks in fostering innovation and growth?
- How can innovative businesses be built and managed in complex and uncertain high-tech environments?
- How can technological entrepreneurship be developed and diffused?

Aldo Romano

Acknowledgements

I would like to gratefully acknowledge a number of people, without whom the completion of this volume would have not been possible. First, I thank Prof. Aldo Romano, who gave me the chance to engage in this project and also Ms Giustina Secundo for her ongoing and excellent work in organizing the eBMS's Advanced International Summer School, that has exposed me to the distinguished contributors of this work. Then, special gratitude goes to Professors Pierpaolo Andriani, Ernesto Damiani, Giuseppina Passiante and Andrea Prencipe, for having organized and led the research tracks and discussions in which most of the insights in this volume were collected. And last, but not least, Dr Alessandro Margherita for his enthusiasm and support.

Claudio Petti

Introduction

Technological entrepreneurship combines two main concepts. The first is technology, which is 'the theoretical and practical knowledge, skills, and artifacts that can be used to develop products and services as well as their production and delivery systems' (Burgelman et al., 2004, p. 2). The second is entrepreneurship, which can be defined as 'the identification and exploitation of previously unexploited opportunities through the creation of new resources or the combinations of existing resources in new ways, to develop and commercialize new products, move into new markets and/or service new customers' (Hitt et al., 2001, p. 480).

According to these combined definitions, technological entrepreneurship can be conceived as recognizing, discovering and even creating entrepreneurial opportunities from technological developments. Entrepreneurial opportunities are the possibilities to create future economic artifacts originating from the divergence of beliefs towards the future value of resources – technologies in our case – given the possibility to transform them in future outputs, that is, technological applications (Kirzner, 1997; Venkatraman and Sarasvathy, 2001). Thus, (Casson, 1982) entrepreneurial opportunities are 'those situations in which new goods, services, raw materials, and organizing methods can be introduced and sold at greater than their costs of production' and differ from the larger set of opportunities to create profits as they require the discovery of new means-ends relationships, as opposed to optimization within existing means-ends frameworks (Kirzner, 1997).

Despite the number of success stories and available cases, new means-ends relationships such as this are not necessarily discovered by serendipitous entrepreneurs. Rather, their identification is often the result of a conscious and systematic entrepreneurial and collective action that transforms the opportunities arising in practical applications and economic and societal value. As a consequence, technological entrepreneurship is referred to herein as a matching process between imagination and needs and, most of all, as a process. In this perspective technological entrepreneurship is not something that results (mainly) from talented minds, but rather is the result of a combination of conscious individual and collective actions within appropriate conditions where talented individuals can optimally contribute. These various conditions, as opposed to inherited individual traits, are something than can be acted upon and ultimately managed and given direction.

This is the rationale underlying the definition of technological entrepreneurship as the process that bridges technology development and business creation, from the recognition or even the creation of potential business value of new discoveries and technologies, to the matching with existing and/or potential market needs, and finally the transformation of opportunities arising in commercial products, services and new businesses.

According to these considerations, technological entrepreneurship has thus three main components, which are:

- An entrepreneurial component, which is the set of actions that individuals and firms perform to identify and harness the distinctive and disruptive potential of emerging technologies and business opportunities that may not be obvious to others.
- A management component, which refers to the actions done by individuals and firms to develop a compelling value proposition capable of rapidly entering a market, possibly with a proven business model, to exploit business opportunities identified.
- An environmental component, which is a set of formal and informal supporting institutions and resources that create the appropriate conditions for technology-based ventures. These factors include public policies, laws and regulations, industry standards and resource endowments (including human capital), knowledge-intensive enterprises and activities, supportive public or public-private institutions, cultures, communities and inter-organizational links.

To summarize, technological entrepreneurship can be assimilated into a type of 'entrepreneurial management' (Stevenson and Jarillo, 1990) – 'all management actions and decisions concerning the creation of new businesses and the related development of innovations from new or reconfigured resources, regardless of the scope of such development efforts (from small start-ups to large, established firms)' (Day, 1992, p. 117). This phenomenon occurs at the intersection of technology development (science and engineering) and business creation (management and business) involving individuals, businesses and governments that transform new ideas into economic and societal value. Such 'entrepreneurial management' functions in an innovative firm are discussed in the contribution by Lazonick (Chapter 1, this volume).

The technological entrepreneurship process incorporates four main sets of activities related to: the creation of new technologies or the identification of existing (but previously unexploited) technologies; the recognition and matching opportunities arising from applications of these technologies to emerging market needs; technology/applications development; and business creation.

1. The creation or identification of technologies involves the recognition of relationships and connections that lead to discoveries (revealing something that was unknown) and inventions (the possible applications of discoveries into the real world). Regarding technology creation, Allen (2003) offers a straightforward explication of the aforementioned activities, using the example of the design of the canal systems for the city of Florence in Italy by Leonardo da Vinci. Allen notes that the relationship/connection da Vinci made was that canals might be compared to tree branches. He studied how nutrients and water flows in tree branches and discovered, through extrapolation, how water flows through canals. This understanding was the stimulus to the invention of a hydraulic device that controlled water levels in canals. This new theoretical and practical body of knowledge, skills and artifacts (this 'technology') then became applied generally, for example, in wind and water-powered mills. This example also suggests that the creation of new technologies is characterized by both creative and structured basic and applied research activities that involve thinking and insight (the relationship/connection between canals and tree branches) as well as generating and codifying new knowledge (how nutrients and water flows into tree branches and the functioning of canal systems) and solving particular technical problems (control water levels so that boats can pass under bridges). As for the identification of existing and previously unexploited technologies, value creation opportunities do not necessarily result from new technologies. Existing and previously unexploited technologies may also be an important trigger for the technological entrepreneurship process. To understand the relevance of these factors, one can refer to the study by Rivette and Kline (2000) who noted that IBM's systematic exploitation of its existing intellectual property resulted in increases in its annual royalty stream by 33 times in ten years. To achieve the same results in terms of profits, the authors estimated that IBM would have to increase worldwide sales by approximately one-fourth each year (an additional $20 billion of products). Moreover, as Wasserman shows in Chapter 6, a technology such as open source might generate a number of very different ways to create value.

Whether via creation and identification, the outcomes are technologies that can be used to develop products and services as well as their production and delivery systems (that is, applications).

2. The second set of activities involves the recognition of opportunities to match the potential applications of the technology created/identified with a market need or space – that is, a business opportunity – and decide about IP securing and protection to ensure the potential of value creation. In this context, recognition means both the identification of an existing need in the marketplace and a way to satisfy that need (for example, genetically modifying a plant to increase crop production), as well as the creation of demand for something people did not previously understand they needed (for example, mobile phones). There are a number of sources from which such business opportunities can be identified: applied research activities, familiar industries and businesses, social and professional networks, customers, universities' technology transfer offices and government agencies. In this volume, there are a number of contributions that address these issues:

    ● Cobis (Chapter 2) addresses the policy-making approach, scientific research supporting mechanisms and related areas of actions of the Italian Ministry of Education, University and Research (MIUR).
    ● Verrill (Chapter 3) discusses the role of universities for the transfer of research results into meaningful enterprises by presenting strategies used by the Massachusetts Institute of Technology (MIT), such as the 60-year-old Industrial Liaison Program, the Technology Licensing Office, and a set of dedicated centers and initiatives.
    ● Hulsink, Elfring and Stam (Chapter 5) analyse the effect of networks and relationships in the discovery and development of innovations by drawing on empirical results described in the literature over the past ten years.

Business opportunities arising from technologies created/identified are often reflected in a business concept that is the main output of this phase. It represents a necessary bridge between the idea(s) for the application(s) of the technology and feasible business(es). It is a necessary tool to test the market feasibility of the opportunity(ies) identified. Understanding the relevance of this activity is similar to trying to understand why so many technologies and applications are never commercialized, without talking about commercial success. The business concept is the key to undertaking the transformation of an idea into real value, of imagination into realization. Following Allen (2003), the business concept offers a formal description of an opportunity composed of four elements: the product/service being offered, the target customer, the value proposition (that is, the benefits for the customer) and the means by which those benefits will be delivered to the customers (or distribution). The business concept, including a plan of how the business will make money and create value for its customers and partners, creates a business model. Similarly, a common mistake of aspiring entrepreneurs is to stick to a logical or default business model without considering the many other ways that revenues can be generated from the same technology. In this regard, Wasserman (Chapter 6) identifies as many as 11 business models for open source software.

Most of the time, value creation is a matter of doing things differently, innovating the business concepts and models or creating completely new ones, such as in the case of Eurotech Group, reported in Siagri, Barbaro and Buttolo (Chapter 7). Eurotech Group developed an innovative multi-option strategy, based on balancing exploitation and exploration of technologies/innovations and leveraging of knowledge networks that allowed the company to manage multiple business models. Eurotech Group became a 'pocket multinational', as defined by the authors, active on a global scale (in Europe, North America and Asia) with a compounded annual growth rate (CAGR) of more than 55 per cent over the last five years.

3. The process of developing activities begins after a business concept has been successfully tested and a feasible business opportunity has been identified. This process is described here as product and related business model design, development and prototyping. The goal is to test the technical and commercial feasibility of the technology/application and decide whether to license it, to sell it or to create a new company for its exploitation. If successful, the result of these activities is a technological application. Innovation and product development literature is full of such insights and cases. This volume will not particularly focus on these issues, as the contributions are directed more towards the task of determining and instituting the most appropriate system, and the organizational and individual level conditions for ensuring a successful transformation of ideas and opportunities into commercial success, rather than on the management of the process itself.

4. Finally, the process most often concludes with the creation of a new company that utilizes the technology/application developed to create new business (and societal value) that is the final outcome of this set of activities and the main rationale for the technology entrepreneurship process. This moves into topics related to the set-up, organization, equipping and financing (thereby, evaluation)

of a new technology-based venture. As such, the contributions of this monographs offer a number of insights related to:

- Financing actors and dynamics as in Verrill's (Chapter 3) and Olivier's (Chapter 4) contributions, who describe the role of angel funds in sustaining the first steps of a technology-based venture.
- The issues and mechanisms regarding the evaluation of ventures such as those mentioned in Siagri, Barbaro and Buttolo's contribution (Chapter 7).
- The human capital needs of new business developments, described in the contribution of Harris (Chapter 8) that details a joint initiative between Intel and UCLA Berkeley to spur entrepreneurship capabilities, and also its effect on economic development and social well-being, as in the contribution of Lazonick (Chapter 1) who discusses the role of system-level factors such as basic educational levels and 'brain circulation' that are the fundamental engines of growth and development of the 'Silicon Valleys' and 'Route 128s' around the world, reporting on the cases of Japan, South Korea, Malaysia, Taiwan, India and China.

A number of actors with various diverse and overlapping roles are involved in the process of making an 'entrepreneurial ecosystem' that is composed of a network of:

- interacting individuals, that is, academics, engineers, entrepreneurs, company managers, civil servants and new graduates;
- companies, such as Eurotech (Chapter 7) or Intel (Chapter 8);
- academic and research institutions, such as UCLA Berkeley (Chapter 8) or the Technology Licensing Office and the Deshpande Center at MIT (Chapter 3);
- government ministries and/or agencies involved in technology transfer, such as the Ministry of Education, University and Research in Italy or the Ministry of Education, Culture, Sports, Science and Technology in Japan (Chapter 2) or mission-oriented international organizations, such as the United Nations Industrial Development Organization;
- private investors, including business angels like the BAMS Angels Fund (Chapter 4); and
- other organizations, which include non-profit organizations/ movements, such as the Free Software Foundation or the Open Source Initiative (Chapter 6).

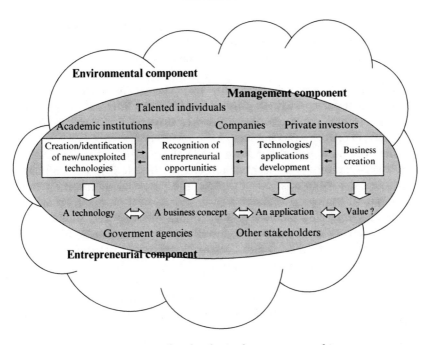

Figure 1   A systemic view of technological entrepreneurship.

Figure 1 represents the aforementioned considerations of technological entrepreneurship as related to its components, activities, outputs and actors.

This volume attempts to shed light on some practical issues related to the underpinnings of the functioning of such a system by discussing a number of experiences and field insights on how various elements interrelate within the technological entrepreneurship process. These elements affect different actors (from government bodies to private investors and companies), at different levels (national policies, networks and collaborations, single companies) and at different stages in their life cycle (from start-up to incumbents), in Europe as well as in the USA. More specifically, the main themes of the cases and empirical analyses reported in this volume are:

- the role of entrepreneurship and innovation for economic growth and social well-being;
- the role of governments, universities and private investors in starting and supporting this process;
- the role of networks as the fuse and the fuel in discovery and innovation;

- some possible business models for transforming technological innovations into profits; and
- the diffusion of technological entrepreneurship culture and skills.

Table 1 reports a synthesis of the main issues (in rows) related to technological entrepreneurship as discussed in the different chapters (in columns) to help the reader identify where they can find cases, examples and insights related to such issues.

This volume is useful for both academics and practitioners in that it presents a range of concepts combined with practical and empirical origins of contributions. Nevertheless, the potential of fostering both economic growth and societal well-being, as well as the difficulty of converting emerging technologies into both business and social value, makes this work most useful to international practitioners. In particular, it is most useful to those practitioners fostering and practicing techno-logical entrepreneurship for and/or inside organizations in Europe and in emerging economies who address such questions as 'Where do good ideas come from? What is a good idea? How do ideas become opportu-nities? How do I seize a business opportunity? Where and how do I get money?'

The experiences and field analysis presented herein represent good sources for scholars teaching technology and innovation management, economics of innovation, strategic management of technology and innovation.

CHAPTER OVERVIEW

This volume is a collection of eight contributions whose contents are sum-marized below.

In Chapter 1 William Lazonick identifies the roles of entrepreneur-ship in the formation of new firms and identifies the basic roles of the entrepreneur. Examples are used to point out that in the advanced economies successful entrepreneurship in knowledge-intensive industries has depended heavily upon a combination of two factors: (1) business allocation of resources to innovative investment strategies, and (2) gov-ernment investment in the knowledge base, state-sponsored protection of markets and intellectual property rights and state subsidies to support these business strategies. National economic development is explained through the interaction of the 'developmental state' and the dynamics of innovative enterprise that makes entrepreneurial activity an important engine for the process of economic development as related to a number

Table 1 *Monograph concept map*

Issues	Chapter 1	Chapter 2	Chapter 3	Chapter 4	Chapter 5	Chapter 6	Chapter 7	Chapter 8
Creating new technologies (through research)		X						
Identifying and exploiting existing technologies						X	X	
Developing value proposition and business model			X			X	X	
Devising a set of formal and informal institutions	X	X						
Leveraging collaboration and social networks		X	X		X	X	X	
Innovating business concepts/models					X	X	X	
Setting up, funding and growing new company		X	X	X		X	X	
Valuing a technology-based venture							X	
Generating impacts and effects on economic development	X		X					X
Developing knowledge, human capital and networks	X	X			X			X
Developing and diffusing entrepreneurship			X					X
Entrepreneurs' role	X	X	X					
Governments' role	X	X						
Universities' role			X					
Private investors' role			X	X				

of cases in developed (USA, Italy and Japan) as well as in developing countries (India, China and the Asian Tigers), in high-tech (for example, biotechnology) and more traditional sectors (for example, textiles and machinery).

In Chapter 2 Fabrizio Cobis analyses recent public policies of France, Japan and especially Italy, and advocates for the emergence of a new model of innovation based on a constant and thorough interaction among enterprises, universities and government institutions. The action of these three subjects is depicted as a sort of 'triple helix'. The ways in which this approach are being applied is described in a thorough analysis of MIUR's policies, especially related to the model of technological districts and the procedures followed for their concrete realization.

David Verrill in Chapter 3 describes the role and mechanisms of universities like MIT as important engines of innovation and business creation for the areas in which they are located. The Boston/Cambridge area example is used to discuss the ingredients that make such areas a dynamic ecosystem of innovation and the roles of the different actors in such ecosystems. Finally, the research areas for great innovations are highlighted with the analysis of venture capital investment.

In Chapter 4 Maurice Olivier draws on lessons learned with the BAMS Angel Fund in Belgium and parallel experience with a similar fund in the USA to explore why collectively organized angel groups may be more effective in responding to the needs of 'late early stage' (or 'first stage') start-up companies.

The premise is that these groups can harness the collective wealth, wisdom, knowledge, talent, time available and commitment of a larger group of motivated individuals who – in addition to positioning themselves naturally in the €0.7–2.5 million investment 'equity gap' range – are able and willing to mentor and guide the management of the investee companies. Conditions for success include subtle leadership of the group by dedicated leaders, clear structures and rules, empowerment, mutual respect, cross-fertilization, professionalism, available templates and models, the ability to converge and decide quickly on important issues, and, last but not least, the important factors of friendship and fun.

In Chapter 5 Willem Hulsink with Tom Elfring and Wouter Stam discuss key network concepts, such as social capital, relational embeddedness (strong and weak ties), structural embeddedness (structural holes) and a number of empirical analyses collected in relevant literature developed over the last ten years. They identify the central role of knowledge in the discovery and realization of innovations, social networks and their potential for knowledge brokering and the relationship between particular network characteristics and innovation.

Tony Wassermann in Chapter 6 addresses the case of open source software to discuss a wide variety of business models that have been used, including dual-licensing, professional services and support, and multiple product lines. Each of these models is described, along with examples of companies that are following each approach and some insights for choosing the appropriate business models for launching a new business in this field.

In Chapter 7 Roberto Siagri with Andrea Barbaro and Nicola Buttolo illustrate the multi-option strategy used at Eurotech Group to develop and sustain its business model(s). In particular, after reviewing the characteristics and advantages of the different mechanisms at the basis of Eurotech's multi-option strategy, the company's strategy is presented as a new high-tech company paradigm driven by systematic value-based scenarios of the future, upon which related optimal strategies are designed and executed in an organizational setting able to manage different and multiple portfolios of options.

Finally, in Chapter 8 Mark Harris, starting from the technical and entrepreneurial shortage of science-based professionals, presents a detailed joint program between Intel and UCLA Berkeley that focuses on accelerating the rate of innovation and economic growth in key markets around the world via the diffusion of entrepreneurship culture and skills in academic faculties.

REFERENCES

Allen, K.R. (2003), *Bringing New Technology to Market*, Upper Saddle River, NJ: Prentice Hall.

Burgelman, R.A., C.M. Christensen and S.C. Wheelwright (2004), *Strategic Management of Technology and Innovation,* New York: McGraw Hill.

Casson, M. (1982), *The Entrepreneur*, Totowa, NJ: Barnes & Noble Books.

Day, D. (1992), 'Research linkages between entrepreneurship and strategic management', in L. Sexton and J.D. Kasarda (eds), *The State of the Art of Entrepreneurship*, Boston, MA: PWS-Kent, pp. 117–63.

Hitt, M.A., R.D. Ireland, S.M. Camp and D.L. Sexton (2001), 'Strategic entrepreneurship: entrepreneurial strategies for wealth creation', *Strategic Management Journal*, **22** (special issue), 479–91.

Kirzner, I. (1997), 'Entrepreneurial discovery and the competitive market process: an Austrian approach', *Journal of Economic Literature*, **36**, 60–85.

Rivette, K.G. and D. Kline (2000), 'Discovering new value in intellectual property', *Harvard Business Review*, **78** (1), 54.

Romano, A., G. Passiante and C.Petti (2003), 'Recent Approaches to Strategic Entrepreneurship', proceedings of the International Entrepreneurship Forum, 3rd International Conference on Entrepreneurial Innovation, 6–8 March, Bangalore, India, pp. 465–77.

Stevenson, H. and J.C. Jarillo (1990), 'A paradigm of entrepreneurship: entrepreneurial management', *Strategic Management Journal*, **11**, 17–27.
Venkatraman, S. and S.D. Sarasvathy (2001), 'Strategy and entrepreneurship: outlines of an untold story', in M.A. Hitt, E. Freema and J.S. Harrison, *Handbook of Strategic Management*, Blackwell, Oxford, pp. 650–68.

1. Entrepreneurship, innovative enterprise and economic development

William Lazonick

TWO WORLDS OF ENTREPRENEURSHIP

In recent years development agencies as well as politicians have called for policies that can encourage 'entrepreneurship' in the poorest parts of the world with a view to closing the ever-growing gap between regions that have and regions that have not (UNDP, 2004; World Bank, 2004; Utomi, 2006). The term 'entrepreneurship' is often used rather loosely to mean any instance in which an individual takes the initiative to do something new and constructive, whether in the sphere of business, government or civil society. Nevertheless, there appears to be a general consensus that the type of entrepreneurship that makes a direct contribution to economic development is that which entails the founding of a new business enterprise. New firm formation, it is thought, tends to allocate the economy's resources to more productive uses than would otherwise have been the case.

Yet at any point in time, the vast majority of the business sector output of an economy derives from the investment and employment of established firms. As in the late 1990s dot.com binge in the advanced economies, the founding of new firms may actually waste an economy's productive resources rather than enlarge them. Under these circumstances, entrepreneurship may be 'value-reducing', and through the manipulation of the stock market even 'value-extracting' rather than 'value-creating'. For entrepreneurship to contribute to economic development, a new firm must transform productive resources into valued outputs in ways that existing firms are unable or unwilling to do.

Within the history of economic thought, the idea that entrepreneurship can make important, and even fundamental, contributions to economic development can be found in its most explicit and forceful form in the early work, now almost a century old, of the Austrian economist, Joseph Schumpeter (1934; also Schumpeter, 1950, 1965). The current interest among development practitioners in the promise of entrepreneurship, however, stems less from the rediscovery of Schumpeter and more from experiences in new firm formation at the extreme ends of the enormous global divide between the rich and the poor.

On the rich side of the entrepreneurial divide, there is the success of the USA in high-tech industries, most notably microelectronics, in which start-ups have played conspicuous roles. From the 1960s, a new breed of venture capitalist, many with prior managerial or technical experience in the semi-conductor industry, backed so many microelectronics startups clustered in the region around Stanford University that by the early 1970s the district was dubbed 'Silicon Valley'. Innovation in semiconductors, and especially the development of the microprocessor – in effect a computer on a chip – created the basis for the emergence of the microcomputer industry from the late 1970s, which in turn resulted in the enormous growth of an installed base of powerful 'hosts' in homes and offices that made possible the Internet revolution of the 1990s. At each stage, entrepreneurs, often backed by venture capitalists, launched new firms, many of which failed but some of which drove the further evolution of the microelectronics revolution.

On the poor side of the entrepreneurial divide are the millions of new firms, typically consisting of only the entrepreneur herself, that have had access to microfinance provided by the Grameen bank in Bangladesh as well as its many imitators in poor countries around the world. Begun as an experiment in the last half of the 1970s, Grameen is a cooperative bank that makes collateral-less loans to the poor to enable them to employ themselves in income-generating activities, most of which rely on their existing skills and physical resources. In 1979 Grameen lent US$180 000 to 2200 bank members, 41 per cent of whom were women. In 2007 it lent US$731 million to 7.4 million members, 97 per cent of whom were women.[1] While there have been debates on the extent to which these loans contain subsidies as well as on the reasons why the loan recipients are almost all female (Wahid, 1994; Hashemi et al., 1996; Hossain, 2002, Mallick, 2002), there is no doubt that the Grameen experiment in entrepreneurship has resulted in the productive use of previously underemployed human resources and augmented the standards of living of the borrowers.

The UNDP report, 'Unleashing entrepreneurship', acknowledges the relevance of these two worlds of entrepreneurship (defined very broadly) when it states: 'Entrepreneurship encompasses the actions of small, informal, village-based individuals as much as it does that of the managers and innovators in multinational corporations and large local companies' (UNDP, 2004, Foreword). Nevertheless, the two extreme examples of entrepreneurship in Bangladesh and the USA that I have cited are worlds apart in terms of both context and impact. The challenge for the poorer countries is to find ways to start firms that can climb the 'value-added' ladder, and make larger and more sustaining contributions to the development of the economy. From this perspective, it is reasonable to expect that policy-makers who believe that entrepreneurship is important to economic development would want to have a thorough understanding of the developmental dynamics that have characterized a region grown rich like Silicon Valley. Indeed, given the importance of the microelectronics industry to the rapid growth of the newly industrializing economies of East Asia, the case of Silicon Valley would seem to be a logical starting point for a comparative-historical analysis of the role, spread and impact of high-tech entrepreneurship around the world.

In this chapter I consider the role of entrepreneurship in the development process within a theory of innovative enterprise that recognizes the complementary, and in many ways more fundamental, contributions of what some have called the 'developmental state'. The next section explores the nature of the entrepreneurial functions. The following section then considers the role of entrepreneurship and innovative enterprise within the nation-state.

THE ENTREPRENEURIAL FUNCTIONS IN THE INNOVATING FIRM

What role, then, does entrepreneurship play in the innovation process, and what are the implications for understanding how the entrepreneurial function is performed? We can provide some answers to these questions by considering the role of the entrepreneur in the performance of the firm's three generic activities: strategy, organization and finance. We want to understand the ability and incentive of the entrepreneur to engage in:

1. The exercise of strategic control by allocating resources to an innovative investment strategy.
2. The management of organizational integration by creating incentives for the individuals who participate in the firm's hierarchical and functional division of labor to supply their skills and efforts to the innovation process.
3. The mobilization of financial commitment by assuring that the firm has a continuous supply of financial resources available to sustain the innovation process until it can generate financial returns.

If it were the case that the entrepreneur could generate innovation as an isolated individual, then she could make the strategic decision to allocate resources to the innovation process, organize her own skill and effort to engage in the learning that is the essence of innovation, and commit her own financial resources to sustaining the innovation process until she generated a higher quality, lower cost product that could generate financial returns. Isolated innovation is, however, rarely the case. In general, the entrepreneur must secure the cooperation of other people who possess specialized labor and sufficient finance in order to transform strategic investment decisions into innovative products. In doing so, as we shall see, the entrepreneur typically must share strategic control.

The entrepreneur is first and foremost a strategist. She makes strategic investment decisions depending on the particular product market in which she wishes to compete and the particular productive activities that, in her view, will enable her firm to generate competitive products. As we have seen, these investment decisions must be made in the face of technological, market and competitive uncertainty.

While we can expect that an element of inexplicable 'luck' will enter into the success or failure of entrepreneurship, research also shows that the successful entrepreneur is a person who confronts uncertainty with considerable career experience in and knowledge of a segment of an industry to which she has in essence dedicated her life. Studies of what Gompers et al. (2005) have called 'entrepreneurial spawning' show unequivocally that entrepreneurial activity in high-tech sectors is knowledge-intensive and industry-specific (see also Shane, 2000; Klepper, 2001; Feldman et al., 2005; Porter et al., 2005). The relevance of the career paths of entrepreneurs for developing economies is also evident in the work of AnnaLee Saxenian (2006) on the 'brain circulation' of Taiwanese, Chinese and Indian scientists, engineers and managers who have returned to their homelands to found new high-tech firms after gaining graduate education and (often substantial) work experience in the USA. Depending on the locus of learning that is relevant to a particular industry as well as the stage of development of that industry, its entrepreneurs may have had prior career experience in established companies, other young companies, research institutes or academia. The important point is that the career paths of entrepreneurs who populate an industry are not random and, hence, relative to the general population, their capacity to confront and overcome uncertainty is not simply a matter of luck.

Within a particular industry in a particular time and place, the vast majority of people whose career paths could lead them to engage in entrepreneurship do not aspire to that role. What distinguishes the psychological makeup of the risk-taking entrepreneur from others equally well-placed who do not take up the challenge is probably the most difficult of the determinants of entrepreneurship to document empirically (Shane,

2003, ch. 5). Insofar as there is a 'classical' debate in the literature on entrepreneurship, it is whether it is the psychological traits of the entrepreneur or objective conditions, career experience and one's location in time and place that are more important in determining the quantity and quality of entrepreneurship that is forthcoming. In a far-reaching survey of 'the sociology of entrepreneurship', in which entrepreneurship is defined as 'the creation of new organizations', Patricia Thornton (1999, p. 19) argues that '[u]ntil recently, the supply-side perspective, which focuses on the individual traits of entrepreneurs, has been the dominant school of research [whereas] [n]ewer work from the demand-side perspective has focused on . . . the context within which entrepreneurship occurs'.

In a theory of innovative enterprise, the key 'supply-side' issue is the capability of the entrepreneur to go beyond the launching of a new venture to contribute to its transformation into a going concern. For a person who makes the strategic decision to become an entrepreneur by founding an innovating firm, the test of her suitability for an ongoing role in the innovation process will come when she tries to build an organization to develop products and processes that will, she hopes, become sources of the firm's innovative success. Unless the new firm is a one-person consultancy, the entrepreneur will find herself playing the role of organizer of other people's labor, and even a very small firm in a knowledge-intensive industry can grow quickly to, say, 30 employees. In the innovating firm, moreover, the organizational challenge is not one of keeping easily replaceable employees at work on routine tasks. The innovating firm makes strategic investments in the employment of a significant number of highly capable specialists, who typically have attractive alternative opportunities but whose labor services must be integrated into the firm's collective and cumulative learning process in order to generate innovation.

Some entrepreneurs may have an aptitude for running a learning organization, especially those who have had experience as managers in established companies. In high-tech industries, however, it is often the case that the innovating firm will employ professional managers with experience and accomplishments in the industry concerned to run its day-to-day operations. The success of organizational learning generally depends on an ongoing process of strategic investment as old problems are solved and new problems are discovered. It is, therefore, typically necessary for the hired managers to be included, along with the entrepreneur, in the strategic decision-making process. Yet, often reluctant to share strategic control of the firms that they have founded, many entrepreneurs resist employing professional managers, a stance that almost invariably is detrimental to the innovation process.

Also detrimental to the innovation process is the interfirm mobility of the specialized labor that the firm employs. Especially in a new venture that, with a relatively small number of people, is striving to integrate the specialized capabilities of highly qualified individuals into a collective and cumulative learning process, the departure of even a few employees can have a devastating impact. The problem of highly mobile labor is particularly the case in US high-tech districts such as Silicon Valley or Boston's Route 128 where, especially in a boom, large numbers of startups spring up in close proximity to existing firms in the industry to try to take advantage of the entrepreneurial opportunity.

Yet, while labor market mobility poses a major managerial problem for the new venture, without that mobility the new venture would not have been able to gain access to this specialized labor in the first place. The types of people that a knowledge-intensive startup wishes to recruit typically have alternative opportunities in established organizations. Relative to the secure employment that these established organizations typically offer, employment at a new venture is inherently insecure.

How then do new ventures attract the quantity and quality of 'talent' that they need to implement their innovative strategies? From the 1960s Silicon Valley high-tech firms began using 'broad-based' employee stock options as the mode of compensation to attract personnel (Lazonick, 2003; Glimstedt et al., 2006). Especially from the 1980s most Silicon Valley high-tech startups have offered stock options to virtually all of their employees – hence the term 'broad-based'. A new venture often grants stock options to employees in lieu of a portion of the salary that they could have commanded working for an established organization, and thus conserves cash. Moreover, those individuals who are deemed to be 'stars' can be offered an extra large number of options as a signing bonus without upsetting the firm's normal salary scale or requiring the firm to expend cash upfront.

Nevertheless, the point of employee stock options, just as the point of human resource management more generally, is not simply to attract specialized labor or save on salaried compensation. Given the collective and cumulative character of the learning process, once an employee is hired the entrepreneur (or her managers) has to retain them, and having retained them, continuously motivate them. In a new venture, employee stock options help to perform both the retention and motivation functions.

So that stock options will perform the retention function, it is the practice in US high-tech for a block of options granted in any given year to vest in equal proportions at the end of each of the four following years. Once the options have vested, the employee has the right to exercise these options over a period of ten years from the original grant date. Thus the employee must stay with the firm for a period of time to have the prospect of cashing in on her stock options. Furthermore, the practice in US high-tech firms is to grant stock options on an annual basis, so that the employee always has more options waiting to vest and eligible to be exercised in the pipeline.

Besides attracting and retaining specialized employees, the entrepreneur has to motivate them to engage in an intense process of organizational learning. Established business enterprises can use the realistic promise of promotion within the organization over the course of a career to perform the motivation function. New ventures cannot realistically proffer such an expectation. In a new venture broad-based stock options can perform this motivation function giving the employees who hold them a strong incentive to contribute to the innovation process. The financial reward for their time and effort will come if and when the new venture has sufficiently developed and utilized its productive resources to do an initial public offering (IPO) or a private sale of the firm to a company that is already listed on the stock market. At that point the new venture's shares, which, not being traded, had previously been difficult to sell after employees exercised their options, now, having become tradable, can become very valuable.[2]

In a new venture, therefore, stock options can serve as a powerful tool for organizational integration. Stock options also serve, however, to dilute the entrepreneur's ownership stake as they are exercised, and as such manifest the collective character of the innovation process. At the same time, the use of this compensation tool creates an almost irresistible pressure for the firm to do an IPO, thus tying its performance in the minds of the firm's participants to its prospective stock market valuation. One danger is that in a boom the financial opportunity will overwhelm the productive opportunity, as new ventures that have yet to develop a commercializable product go public and are, as a result, exposed to the demands of financial markets for regular returns.

Another related danger of a premature IPO is that those participants in the firm who hold large ownership stakes can, quite legally, gain incredible wealth from the new venture even though the firm whose stock yields them this wealth has not yet succeeded as a viable business enterprise (see Gimein et al., 2002; Carpenter et al., 2003; Lazonick, 2007b). Especially in a speculative environment, the prospect of such gains can in turn attract entrepreneurs into the industry who lack the specialized knowledge of the industry required for innovative strategy, and whose main concern is with cashing in on the new venture whether or not it is a commercial success. Insofar as certain entrepreneurs are able to repeat this process, their 'serial entrepreneurship' may not contribute to innovation in the industry – or industries – in which they are involved.

Of central importance to the success of US venture capital in supporting innovative enterprise has been the fact that many of the leading venture capitalists had themselves followed managerial careers in high-tech industry before becoming purveyors of finance to new high-tech firms. In playing this role, the most successful venture capitalists do more than provide what I have called financial commitment. They also participate in the exercise of strategic control, sitting on the boards of the new ventures that they have helped finance, and they are typically the ones who recruit managers to perform the firm's organizational functions instead of the entrepreneur.

At the same time, as providers of venture finance, their prime objective is not to build the capabilities of, and reap the returns from, one company for the rest of their careers. Rather their aim is to 'exit' the firm at a propitious time in the not too distant future, either by going public with the new ventures in which they have invested or by doing a private sale to an established company. In this context, a well-developed stock market is an institution that permits founder-entrepreneurs and venture capitalists to exit from their investments, quite apart from whether an IPO also raises funds for the firm that has issued its stock. Under these institutional conditions, entrepreneurship may be ephemeral as an input into the innovation process; the entrepreneur disappears as the innovative enterprise lives on.

ENTREPRENEURSHIP IN THE NATION-STATE

An analysis of the functions of entrepreneurship in the innovation process shows that the success or failure of the entrepreneur is highly dependent on the set of social relationships in which she is embedded. The need for organizational integration and financial commitment generally means that the entrepreneur must share strategic control with professional managers and financiers. Large numbers of participants in the firm's hierarchical and functional division of labor need to be motivated to work together for a sustained period of time towards the achievement of collective goals. In the US context, the collective character of the innovation process in new ventures is all the greater when one considers that the vast majority of venture capital funds come from employee pension funds, university endowments, philanthropic foundations and business corporations. Many rich individuals invest directly in new ventures, but such 'angel investing', while of greater importance in the 2000s than previously, is not the norm.

At the level of the business enterprise, the collective character of the innovation process reflects the reliance of the entrepreneur on the skills and efforts of other enterprise participants in the exercise of strategic control, the management of organizational integration and the mobilization of financial commitment. Comparative-historical research on innovative enterprise across advanced nations and over time has revealed

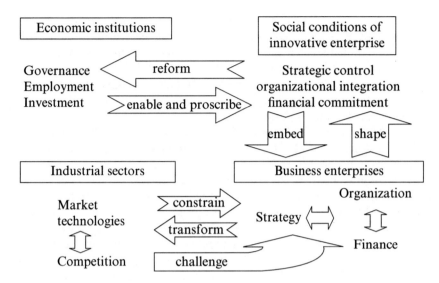

Figure 1.1   Social conditions of innovative enterprises.

distinctive patterns in social structures that support the transformation of strategic control, organizational integration and financial commitment into innovative outcomes (Lazonick, 2007c). As illustrated schematically in Figure 1.1, I call these distinctive social structures 'social conditions of innovative enterprise'. Historically, as particular forms of these social conditions have provided the foundations for the growth of innovative enterprises in a national economy, and as enterprises characterized by these social conditions have grown to dominate resource allocation in the national economy as a whole, these social conditions of innovative enterprise themselves have become national norms for business behavior that have shaped the form and content of national governance, employment and investment institutions.

For example, in the USA of the 2000s, reflecting the rise of what I have called the 'New Economy business model', governance institutions emphasize 'maximizing shareholder value', employment institutions emphasize interfirm labor mobility and stock options, and investment institutions emphasize venture finance and the use of corporate stock to combine with other companies (Lazonick, 2006a). The characteristics of these institutions differ markedly from those that, reflecting the 'Old Economy business model' that prevailed in the post-World War II decades, emphasized corporate growth, career employment with one company and long-term debt finance. By contrast, Japanese economic institutions, although currently under some pressure for change, emphasize stable shareholding, permanent employment and bank-based finance, all of which evolved as social conditions of innovative enterprise in the major Japanese companies that grew to dominate the economy from the 1950s and transformed Japan into a rich nation by the 1980s (Lazonick, 2005).

It is now widely recognized among scholars of comparative political economy that there exists a wide array of 'varieties of capitalism' that can provide the institutional bases for economic development (see Berger and Dore, 1996; Crouch and Streeck, 2001; Hall and Soskice, 2001; Whitley, 2002; Lazonick, 2007c). Moreover, looking back over the past century, the changes in the governance, employment and investment institutions that have characterized the leading capitalist economies have been profound. A century ago Britain still had the highest level of GDP per capita in the world, and one could identify, as indeed Alfred Marshall (1920) did, the industrial districts around Manchester, Sheffield and Birmingham as the reasons why Britain could be known as the 'workshop of the world'. The thousands of relatively small companies that populated these districts produced commodities such as cotton textiles and metal housewares for export to markets around the world. Enterprise governance was based on either proprietorships or, as in the case of cotton spinning, highly localized, single-plant limited liability firms. In the leading export sectors, of which cotton textiles was by far the most important, new ventures used local stock markets to raise funds for rapid investments in new factories to respond to cyclical booms in demand. The foundation for British global supremacy in these industries was the availability of large local supplies of unionized labor with specialized craft skills (see Farnie, 1979; Lazonick, 1983; Farnie and Abe, 2000).

In periods of strong product market demand the ready availability of specialized craft labor induced new specialized manufacturing firms, often started by entrepreneurial craft workers, to set up in these districts. The growth of a district induced other firms to invest in regionally specific communication and distribution facilities for the supply of materials, the transfer of work-in-progress across vertically specialized firms and the marketing of output. Regional concentration encouraged vertical specialization, which in turn eased firm entry into a particular specialty, thus resulting in high levels of horizontal competition. Firms could be owned and managed by the same people, or in the case of the limited liability spinning companies a single manager would direct the one-factory firms. There was no need to invest in the types of managerial organization that by the late nineteenth century were becoming central to the growth of firms, and the development of the economies, of the USA and Germany. In the industrial districts economies of scale were, as Marshall argued, external, rather than internal, to the firm.

By the 1920s, the British industrial districts entered a decline from which they would never recover (Elbaum and Lazonick, 1986). A half century later, however, the remarkable growth of 'the Third Italy', based on industrial districts of small-scale enterprises clustered in Emilia-Romagna around Bologna in Veneto, outside of Venice, and in Tuscany in the vicinity of Florence, led some Italian economists, most notably Giacomo Becattini (1992) and Sebastiano Brusco (1982), to look to the work of Marshall for an analytical framework for understanding the developmental dynamics that these districts possessed. Given the expansion of these industrial districts on the basis of relatively small-scale enterprises, one could rightly point to the role of entrepreneurship as a significant force in the development of the Third Italy. At the same time, a more fundamental analysis of the development of these industrial districts revealed how individual entrepreneurship was embedded in and supported by a highly collective social structure. For example, in an influential essay entitled 'The Emilian model: productive decentralisation and social integration', originally published in Italian in 1980 and translated into English two years later, Brusco (1982, p. 167) presented 'a dynamic analysis of the interaction between the productive structure, the labour market, and the principal political institutions in Emilia-Romagna'.

There were a number of good reasons to refer to the Third Italy as 'Marshallian' industrial districts, as Becattini in particular was wont to do. The industrial activities of these districts focused on, among other things, textiles, footwear and light machinery just as the British districts had done. Each industrial activity was populated by large numbers of vertically specialized proprietary firms in which craft labor was a prime source of competitive advantage and of which many entrepreneurs had previously been craft workers. Yet there were a number of major differences between the nineteenth-century industrial districts that Marshall observed and those that could be found in the Third Italy a generation after the end of World War II. The identification of these differences is of central importance for the analysis of how entrepreneurial activity flourishes, and reaches its limits, in difference social contexts.

The first major difference was the sheer diversity of specialized production by small firms in the Third Italy. Large numbers of the relatively small Italian firms were truly entrepreneurial as, within their specialized industrial activity, firms competed by differentiating their products for higher income and more sophisticated markets. While one could certainly find such entrepreneurial firms in the British industrial districts of the late nineteenth century, those districts and their constituent firms contributed to the growth of the British economy primarily through a system of mass production of standardized goods, even if it was one based on a proliferation of relatively small firms and craft labor.

The second characteristic of the Italian industrial districts that distinguished them from the British districts was the extent to which in Italy collective institutions supported the innovative activities of small firms. In the Italian districts regional universities were important suppliers of both new knowledge and educated labor, quite in contrast to the craft-based provision of these inputs in the British districts. Brusco emphasized the importance of the 'red' local governments in Emilia-Romagna in promoting policies to support the activities of small enterprises, and in particular in facilitating cooperatives that provided these firms with 'real services' related to financing, business administration, marketing and training that they could not provide for themselves and which profit-seeking specialized firms did not find it worthwhile to supply (Brusco and Pezzini, 1990; Brusco, 1992). While consumer cooperatives sprung up in the British industrial districts of the late nineteenth century – with the Lancashire town of Rochdale acquiring fame as the pioneer of the consumer cooperative movement – producer cooperatives were rare.

The third distinguishing characteristic of the Italian industrial districts that became more evident in the 1990s was the extent to which, in some districts and in some industries, 'leading' firms could emerge, drawing on the resources of the industrial districts while, through their own internal growth, transforming the innovative capability of the districts. A problem with the British industrial districts when they were confronted by competitive challenges in the first half of the twentieth century was that dominant firms failed to emerge to lead the restructuring of the districts. Indeed, over the past decade a major concern among many observers of Italian industrial districts has been whether the competitive advantage of regions based on a multitude of small entrepreneurial firms can be maintained when they are confronted by the rise of dominant global enterprises.

In Italy a well-known early case of the emergence of a dominant firm is Benetton, a family firm in the Veneto area, known along with Emilia-Romagna and Tuscany for its industrial districts. Benetton grew from the last half of the 1960s by maintaining control over marketing, design and logistics (including the rapid replenishment of fast-selling shop inventories) while outsourcing production to small producers in its home region (and then increasingly abroad) and establishing a global brand name by franchising retail shops around the world (and subsequently investing in its own 'megashops') (see Harrison, 1994). A similar dynamic of enterprise growth can be found in the rise of Natuzzi, since the early 1990s a leading global brand in upholstered furniture. Based in a newer industrial district in the south of Italy, Natuzzi has combined a tightly integrated vertical supply chain with its own global marketing capabilities to out-compete the more specialized but once dominant furniture manufacturers in Emilia-Romagna (Belussi, 1999). In 2006 Natuzzi had sales of €736 million, and at the end of the year employed 8133 people (3590 in Italy and 4543 abroad).

As demonstrated in the cases of Benetton and Natuzzi, even in industries that are not high-tech, the overwhelming tendency is for entrepreneurial firms to grow large and dominate their industries; one can offer as a particularly well-known example Wal-Mart, the US retailing giant, launched as an entrepreneurial firm in the small town of Bentonville, Arkansas in 1950, that as of January 2007 employed 1.8 million people worldwide, generating $349 billion in revenues and over $11 billion in profits. Another example is the Toyoda Automatic Loom Company, which in the 1920s took advantage of the opportunity for mechanical innovation presented by the rapid growth of the nation's cotton textile industry. By the 1930s Toyoda's weaving innovations had enabled Japan to become the world leader not only in the export of cotton cloth but also in the export of machinery for the weaving of cotton cloth. During the 1930s, moreover, Toyoda strategically transferred its considerable capabilities in mechanical engineering and manufacturing to the development of automobiles under the name of Toyota Motor Company (changing the 'd' to a 't' in the family name so that its customers would not mistake its motor vehicles for its now famous weaving machines) (Mass and Robertson, 1996; Wada, 2006).

Of much greater importance for present purposes, however, is the fact that the growth of Toyota was both central to and emblematic of the transformation of Japan from a poor nation in the 1940s to a rich nation in the 1980s. When in the 1980s and 1990s many 'non-neoclassical' scholars followed Chalmers Johnson (1982) in focusing on the role of the 'developmental state' in the Japanese 'economic miracle', they generally failed to analyse the role of 'innovative enterprise' in this transformation (see Woo-Cumings, 1999). As a direct result, they ignored two fundamental phenomena in the link between entrepreneurship and economic development.

Firstly, they have missed the importance of enterprise strategy, organization and finance in the transformation of entrepreneurial firms into innovative firms. The contribution of the developmental state in Japan to the wealth of the nation cannot be understood in abstraction from the growth of companies such as Toshiba, Hitachi, Toyota, Matsushita, Sony and Canon. While the Japanese state provided various forms of support for these companies, especially in the realm of bank-based finance, it was a combination of strategy, organization and finance internal to these companies that made them successful, and gave the state's industrial policy a chance of reinforcing that success. One needs a theory of innovative enterprise to understand not only the role of entrepreneurship in economic development but also the role of the state.

One can make the same argument for the importance of the growth of dominant firms in the process of economic development for the world's richest economy, the United States. Except, and here is the second phenomenon that Western scholars of the developmental state have entirely missed, in terms of technological innovation over the past century and to the present, the US state has been far more developmental than the Japanese state. Scholarly works have been written on particular industries – for example, agriculture (Ferleger and Lazonick, 1993), airliners (Van der Linden, 2002), aircraft engines (Constant, 1980), computers (National Research Council, 1999), the Internet (Abbate, 2000), biotechnology (Lazonick et al., 2007) – that support this proposition.

As for Silicon Valley, the world's leading high-tech industrial district, the developmental state has been of central importance throughout its history (see Flamm, 1987, 1988; Leslie, 1993a, 1993b; Norberg and O'Neill, 1996; Lécuyer, 2006). In the late 1990s, under the auspices of the US National Research Council (NRC), a group of scholars published *Funding a Revolution: Government Support for Computing Research* (National Research Council, 1999). 'Innovation in computing', the NRC (1999, p. 2) observed,

> stems from a complementary relationship among government, industry, and universities. In this complex arrangement, government agencies and private companies fund research that is incorporated into myriad new products, processes, and services. While the contributions of industry to the computing revolution are manifest in the range of new products, processes, and services offered, those of the federal government are harder to discern. Nevertheless, federal funding of major computing initiatives has often contributed substantially to the development and deployment of commercial technologies. Commercial developments, similarly, have contributed to government endeavors.

In the biotechnology industry, which has been booming in the 2000s, the flow of resources has been much more one way from the government to firms (see Lazonick et al., 2007). Through the National Institutes of Health (NIH), the US government has long been the nation's (and the world's) most important investor in knowledge creation in the medical fields. Since its inception in 1938 through 2007, US tax payers invested $615 billion in 2007 dollars in the work of the NIH, with NIH funding averaging $15.6 billion per year in 1993–97, $21.8 billion per year in 1999–2002 and $29.9 billion per year in 2003–07. The amount of NIH research funds allocated specifically to biotechnology averaged $9.8 billion in 2006 and 2007, down somewhat from an annual average of $10.8 billion in

2004 and 2005. In its 27 centers and institutes in Bethesda, Maryland the NIH supports the medical research of 6000 scientists and technicians. But in-house research absorbs less than 10 per cent of the NIH budget, and administration another 9 per cent. In 2007 NIH awarded $23.7 billion of its $29.2 billion budget for research, training, fellowships and R&D contracts in the form of '50,000 competitive grants to more than 325,000 researchers at over 3,000 universities, medical schools, and other research institutions in every state and around the world'.[3]

The business sector has direct access to, and can appropriate high returns from, this state-funded research. In 1978 intense lobbying by the National Venture Capital Association and the American Electronics Association, both with their centers of gravity as cohesive trade associations in Silicon Valley, convinced the US Congress to lower the capital gains tax rate from 49 per cent to 28 per cent, thus reversing a 36-year trend towards higher capital gains taxes. The Bayh-Dole Act of 1980 gave universities and hospitals clear property rights to new knowledge that resulted from US government-funded research so that they could license the results of their research to new technology firms. The main motivation for Bayh-Dole was the growing number of biotech inventions emanating from NIH research that, it was argued, would be left unexploited but for the Act's less restrictive conditions for the transfer of intellectual property. In 1980 as well a Supreme Court decision that genetically engineered life forms are patentable facilitated the opportunity for the types of knowledge transfers that Bayh-Dole envisioned. The magnitude of the gains that could be reaped from biotech startups became apparent when Genentech, founded in 1976, raised $36 million in its IPO in 1980, to be followed by, at the time, the largest IPO in US history, the $107 million raised by Cetus, another San Francisco Bay area company that dated from 1971.

In 1983 another important inducement to biotech investment followed in the form of the Orphan Drug Act, which gave generous tax credits for research and experimentation as well as the possibility of seven-year market exclusivity for companies that developed drugs for 'rare' diseases. It was argued that without these financial incentives many potential medicinal drugs that could be developed for relatively small markets would remain 'orphans': pharmaceutical or biotech companies would not have been willing to make financial commitments of the size and duration required to nurture these drugs from infancy to adulthood. By December 2006 the FDA had designated 1674 orphan drug submissions that made these companies eligible for the tax credits and had granted market exclusivity on 301 drugs that had reached the approval stage. A number of these orphan drugs are now 'blockbusters' with $1 billion or more in annual sales. The US government, through its Medicare and Medicaid programs, moreover, remains the leading source of effective demand for these high-priced biotech products.

In sum, the USA has had, and still possesses, a formidable developmental state. As for Japan, it was able to grow rich without its state being as developmental as that of the USA precisely because its firms could take advantage, through licensing and joint ventures, of knowledge created in the USA and other advanced Western nations. Nevertheless, the further development and utilization of this knowledge to engage in indigenous innovation required that the Japanese firms have sufficient 'absorptive capacity'.[4] The cases of the Toyoda automatic loom and the Toyota automobile, already mentioned, are examples of such indigenous innovation.

To have this absorptive capacity and engage in indigenous innovation, a nation has to have already made the most strategic and most expensive investment of all: investment in a public system of primary, secondary and tertiary education. The economic institutions that support entrepreneurship and innovation in the USA and Japan may differ radically, but what these as well as other advanced economies have in common are long histories of massive investments in their educational systems.

US government investment began with the Morrill Land Grant Act of 1862, out of which emerged a nationwide system of higher education oriented towards industrial development, including universities such as MIT, Cornell, Michigan, Purdue, Iowa and the University of California Berkeley (Ferleger and Lazonick, 1994). In the development of Silicon Valley, the key player was Stanford University, a private university founded in 1885 on the basis of railroad wealth. From the 1930s Stanford oriented itself to support industrial development. The key 'public entrepreneur' was Frederick Terman. With an electrical engineering doctorate from MIT, Terman was a professor of engineering at Stanford in the 1930s, spent World War II directing the Harvard University Radio Research Lab, returned to Stanford after the war as its dean of engineering and became the University's provost in the 1950s. Two of Terman's students in the 1930s were William Hewlett and David Packard, who in 1939, on the urging of Terman, founded the eponymous firm adjacent to Stanford.

The founding of Hewlett-Packard (HP) reflected Terman's vision of Stanford as a high-tech industrial district that would spawn startups (Leslie and Kargon, 1996). In the Boston area Georges Doriot, a professor at Harvard Business School, had a similar vision. After World War II Doriot and a number of academic and business leaders in the Boston area, through the pioneering venture capital firm, American Research & Development, made a conscious and successful attempt to commercialize the military technologies that had accumulated at the Massachusetts

Institute of Technology, by far the most important university in the nation for military research (Hsu and Kenney, 2005). The result by the 1950s was the emergence of 'Route 128' in the Greater Boston area as the world's leading high-tech industrial district.

Highly aware of these efforts on the East Coast, in his 1946–47 Dean's Report of the Stanford School of Engineering, Terman issued a call for the western United States to make use of its institutions of higher education to foster indigenous innovation (quoted in Leslie, 1993a, p. 55).

> The west has long dreamed of an indigenous industry of sufficient magnitude to balance its agricultural resources. The war advanced these hopes and brought to the west the beginning of a great new era of industrialization. A strong and independent industry must, however, develop its own intellectual resources of science and technology, for industrial activity that depends upon imported brains and second-hand ideas cannot hope to be more than a vassal that pays tribute to its overlords, and is permanently condemned to an inferior competitive position.

In the post-World War II decades nations such as Japan, South Korea and Taiwan would adopt precisely this perspective on industrial development, with the education of the population as the foundation.[5] In the case of Japan, laws dating back to 1886 made primary education universally free and compulsory, and by 1909 98 per cent of all school-age children went to primary school (Koike and Inoki, 1990, p. 227–8). Japan also developed a system of higher education from the late nineteenth century that sent its graduates into industry (Yonekawa, 1984). Additionally, also from the late nineteenth century, Japanese companies engaged in the practice of sending university educated employees abroad for extended periods of time to learn about Western technology (see, for example, Fukasaku, 1992). Of utmost importance to Japan's post-World War II development was the fact that for decades Japanese industrial enterprises had made university educated engineers integral to their managerial organizations (Morikawa, 2001, pp.p 62–3).

A major challenge that faced the would-be 'Asian Tigers' was to transform their national educational systems into a foundation for industrial development. In South Korea, as the most dramatic example, average years of schooling of the 15-plus population rose from 7.91 years in 1980 to 10.84 years in 2000, surpassing Japan's 2000 figure of 9.47 years and not far behind the US figure of 12.05 years (Barro and Lee, 2000). By the last half of 1990s South Korea had the highest number of PhDs per capita of any country in the world (Kim and Leslie, 1998, p. 154).

India, a nation with 680 million people aged 15 or over in 2000 compared with South Korea's 37 million, has not invested in such a dramatic transformation of its mass education system. In 1960 the Indian 15-plus population included 72.2 per cent with no schooling, and had on average 1.68 years of schooling. In 2000 India's no-schooling figure remained high at 43.9 per cent, while the average years of schooling figure was only 5.06. Nevertheless in the post-World War II decades, given the size of its population and the legacy of British colonial rule, India did have large numbers of university graduates – so many in fact that as late as the first half of the 1990s India's problem was less brain drain and more the nation's millions of educated unemployed. Over the past decade educated Indians have also been far and away the most numerous of all nationalities in following global career paths to the USA, on temporary work visas and as permanent residents, for graduate education and work experience (see Lazonick, 2006b).

For those nations that made these investments in education, since the 1960s the development strategies of East Asian nations have interacted with the investment strategies of US-based high-tech companies to generate a global labor supply.[6] This process has entailed flows of US capital to East Asian labor as well as flows of East Asian labor to US capital. As a result, new possibilities to pursue high-tech careers, and thereby develop productive capabilities, have opened up to vast numbers of individuals in East Asian nations. Many found the relevant educational programs and work experience in their home countries. But many gained access to education and experience by following global career paths that included study and work abroad, especially in the USA.

For East Asian nations, these global career paths have posed a danger of 'brain drain': the career path could come to an end in the USA (or another advanced economy) rather than in the country where the individual had been born and bred. Education and experience in the USA created, however, valuable 'human capital' that could potentially be lured back home. A major challenge for the East Asian nations has been the creation of domestic employment opportunities, through a combination of foreign direct investment (FDI), strategic government initiatives and the growth of indigenous businesses, to enable the career paths of global nationals to be followed back home, thus transforming a potential 'brain drain' into an actual 'brain gain'.

Historically, FDI by multinational corporations (MNCs) has been an important source of high-tech employment creation in these nations, mainly because even when they have gone to these countries in search of low-wage labor, the MNCs have also employed indigenous scientists, engineers and managers. US MNCs such as Motorola in South Korea from 1967, Intel in Malaysia from 1972 and Texas Instruments in India from 1985 created some of the first attractive opportunities for nationals to pursue high-tech careers at home.

The greatest impact on innovation and development comes, however, from the creation and growth of indigenous firms.[7] When high-tech employment is dependent on MNCs, there are limits to the transfer of high-quality employment to the host nation, whereas indigenous companies maintain strategic control over the location of job creation. Many of the founders of these indigenous companies have been part of the 'reverse brain drain' from the advanced economies (Saxenian, 2006). Some founders and many key employees have followed career paths entirely at home, going from MNCs to indigenous companies.

In the case of South Korea, indigenous investments by government and business rather than FDI have since the late 1980s driven the development of domestic high-tech capabilities. In the 2000s these indigenous investments are creating new opportunities for high-end investment by MNCs in South Korea, including new investments by a company such as Motorola that has been doing business there for almost 40 years. In contrast, in the absence of leading indigenous high-tech companies, Malaysia's growth still remains highly dependent on the upgrading strategies of MNCs such as Intel. Like Motorola in South Korea, Intel originally went to Malaysia in search of low-wage assembly labor in a politically stable country that had made a commitment to mass education. And like Motorola Korea, Intel Malaysia upgraded its capabilities over time, employing a higher proportion of high-skill labor in higher value-added activities at rising wages.

Like Motorola in South Korea and Intel in Malaysia, Texas Instruments (TI) originally went to India in the mid-1980s in search of low-wage labor. TI, however, was not searching for low-skill labor. What first attracted TI to India was the availability of highly educated engineers and programmers, albeit at much lower wages than would have had to be paid in the USA. Over time, TI expanded and upgraded its Indian operations, employing larger numbers of educated labor to design increasingly complex products. Two decades after TI came to India, the nation is experiencing a growth dynamic in which, with both skill levels and wages rising, indigenous companies such as Tata Consultancy Services, Infosys and Wipro are taking the lead, and in which MNCs are being attracted to India more for the high quality of its high-tech labor supply than for its low cost.

A similar process of indigenous innovation has been taking place in China, but with the difference that indigenous Chinese companies such as Lenovo and Founder have emerged to serve the growing Chinese consumer and business markets, and have drawn upon the capital goods expertise of MNCs such as Intel, TI, Motorola and HP to develop higher quality, lower cost products. Some of these companies – Lenovo and Founder are prime examples – have become leading competitors not only in China but also internationally (Lu, 2000; Lu and Lazonick, 2001; Xie and White, 2004). While there are large numbers of Chinese high-tech employees who have acquired higher education and work experience in the USA, the vast majority have been receiving education and experience in China.

Given the growth dynamic that has taken hold in these nations, sheer size ensures that Indians and Chinese will dominate the expansion of the global high-tech labor supply. Combined, the population of India and China is 33 times that of South Korea and Taiwan. India and China have rapidly growing domestic markets that both provide demand for the products of indigenous companies and give their governments leverage with MNCs in gaining access to advanced technology as a condition for FDI. While India and China offer indigenous scientists and engineers rapidly expanding employment opportunities at home, vast numbers of their educated populations are studying and working abroad. Aided by the ongoing liberalization of US immigration policy (impeded just temporarily by the reaction to 9/11), the global career path is much more of a 'mass' phenomenon for Indian and Chinese scientists and engineers than it has been for the Koreans and Taiwanese. History tells us that, following global career paths, more and more Indian and Chinese high-tech labor will migrate back to their countries of origin, where, as Saxenian (2006) has shown, they have been an important source of high-tech entrepreneurship.

The cases of South Korea and Taiwan should give pause to arguments that investments in knowledge-intensive sectors are not of much relevance to the very poor nations such as those in Africa. While most African nations are certainly not well-positioned to compete in high-tech industry, it must be remembered that South Korea's GDP per capita was only 10 per cent of that of the USA in 1960 and 13 per cent in 1970, while that of Taiwan was just 13 per cent in 1960 and 20 per cent in 1970 (Maddison, 2007). In 2003 South Korea's GDP per capita was 54 per cent of that of the USA and Taiwan's 60 per cent. In the 1980s and 1990s through 'indigenous innovation' – improvements on technologies that are transferred from abroad – these nations, like Japan about a quarter century before, transformed themselves from poor nations into rich nations. Now China and India, with one-third of the world's population, are also developing rapidly on the basis of indigenous innovation.

It would be very misleading to attribute the development of China and India to a sudden emergence of entrepreneurship. There is no doubt that entrepreneurship has been unleashed in these nations. It is a phenomenon, however, that is only explicable through an analysis of the changing social conditions of innovative enterprise.

ACKNOWLEDGMENTS

This chapter draws on a working paper of the World Institute of Development Economics Research (WIDER). I am grateful to Wim Naudé for his comments.

NOTES

1. www.grameen-info.org/index.php?option=com_content&task=view&id=177&Itemid=503, accessed 5 November 2008.
2. Besides the time and effort supplied by motivated employees, the value of stock options may be affected to a considerable extent by speculative swings of the stock market that alter the ease with which a new venture can do an IPO or a private sale to an established company. In the USA, over the years from 1990 to 2005 the average length of time from founding to IPO for venture-backed companies ranged from four years for 487 IPOs in 1999 at the peak of the Internet boom to 15 years for 70 IPOs at the depth of the subsequent slump. In 1999 there were 166 private sales of venture-backed companies for average proceeds (in 2005 dollars) of $265.5 million, while in 2002 there were 157 such sales but average proceeds (in 2005 dollars) of only $57.6 million (Ritter, 2006).
3. www.nih.gov/about/budget.htm, http://grants1.nih.gov/grants/award/trends/DistBudget 07.jpg, accessed 5 November 2008.
4. On the concept of 'absorptive capacity', see Cohen and Levinthal (1990).
5. Indeed, in the late 1960s and early 1970s Terman and his disciples were key advisors to the Koreans in the setting up of what became the Korea Advanced Institute of Science and Technology (KAIST) (see Kim and Leslie, 1998).
6. The following draws on Lazonick (2006b).
7. For the relation between entrepreneurial ventures and the developmental state in the software industries of Ireland, Israel and Taiwan, see Breznitz, 2007.

REFERENCES

Abbate, Janet (2000), *Inventing the Internet*, Cambridge, MA: MIT Press.
Barro, Robert J. and Jong-Wha Lee (2000), 'International data on educational attainment: updates and implications', Harvard Center for International Development working paper No. 42, April, appendix data files, accessed 5 November 2008 at www.cid.harvard.edu/ciddata/ciddata.html.
Becattini, Giacomo (1992), 'The Marshallian industrial district as a socio-economic notion', in F. Pyke, G. Becattini and W. Sengenberger (eds), *Industrial Districts and Inter-firm Cooperation in Italy*, Geneva: International Institute for Labour Studies, pp. 37–51.
Belussi, Fiorenza (1999), 'Path-dependency versus industrial dynamics: an analysis of two heterogeneous districts', *Human Systems Management*, **18**, 161–74.
Berger, Suzanne and Ronald Dore (eds) (1996), *National Diversity and Global Capitalism*, Ithaca, NY: Cornell University Press.
Breznitz, Dan (2007), *Innovation and the State: Political Choice and Strategies for Growth in Israel, Taiwan, and Ireland*, New Haven, CT: Yale University Press.

Brusco, Sebastiano (1982), 'The Emilian model: productive decentralisation and social integration', *Cambridge Journal of Economics*, **6** (2), 167–84.

Brusco, Sebastiano (1992), 'Small firms and the provision of real services', in F. Pyke and W. Sengenberger (eds), *Industrial Districts and Local Economic Regeneration*, International Institute for Labour Studies, pp. 177–96.

Brusco, Sebastiano and M. Pezzini (1990), 'Small-scale enterprise in the ideology of the Italian left', in F. Pyke, G. Becattini and W. Sengenberger (eds), *Industrial Districts and Inter-Firm Cooperation in Italy*, Geneva: International Institute for Labour Studies, pp. 142–59.

Carpenter, Marie, William Lazonick and Mary O'Sullivan (2003), 'The stock market and innovative capability in the new economy: the optical networking industry', *Industrial and Corporate Change*, **12** (5), 963–1034.

Cohen, Wesley M. and Daniel A. Levinthal (1990), 'Absorptive capacity: a new perspective on learning and innovation', *Administrative Science Quarterly*, **35** (1), 128–52.

Constant II, Edward W. (1980), *The Origins of the Turbojet Revolution*, Baltimore, MD: Johns Hopkins University Press.

Crouch, Colin and Wolfgang Streeck (eds) (2001), *Political Economy of Modern Capitalism: Mapping Convergence and Diversity*, London: Sage.

Elbaum, Bernard and William Lazonick (eds) (1986), *The Decline of the British Economy*, New York: Oxford University Press.

Farnie, Douglas A. (1979), *The English Cotton Industry and the World Market, 1815–1896*, New York: Oxford University Press.

Farnie, Douglas A. and Takeshi Abe (2000), 'Japan, Lancashire, and the Asian Market of cotton manufacturers, 1980–1990', in Douglas A. Farnie, David J. Jeremy, Tetsuro Nakaoka, John F. Wilson and Takeshi Abe, *Region and Strategy in Britain and Japan: Business in Lancashire and Kansai, 1890–1990*, London and New York: Routledge, pp. 113–57.

Feldman, Maryann P., Johanna Francis and Janet Bercovitz (2005), 'Creating a cluster while building a firm: entrepreneurs and the formation of industrial clusters', *Regional Studies*, **39** (1), 129–41.

Ferleger, Louis and William Lazonick (1993), 'The managerial revolution and the developmental state: the case of US Agriculture', *Business and Economic History*, **22** (2), 67–98.

Ferleger, Louis and William Lazonick (1994), 'Higher education for an innovative economy: land-grant colleges and the managerial revolution in America', *Business and Economic History*, **23** (1), 116–28.

Flamm, Kenneth (1987), *Targeting the Computer: Government Support and International Competition*, Washington, DC: Brookings Institution.

Flamm, Kenneth (1988), *Creating the Computer: Government, Industry, and High-Technology*, Washington, DC: Brookings Institution.

Fukasaku, Tohiko (1992), *Technology and Industrial Development in Pre-War Japan: Mitsubishi Nagasaki Shipyard, 1884–1934*, London: Routledge.

Gimein, M., E. Dash, L. Munoz and J. Sung (2002), 'You bought. They sold. All over corporate America, top execs were cashing in stock even as their companies were tanking. Who was left holding the bag? You', *Fortune*, 2 September.

Glimstedt, Henrik, William Lazonick and Hao Xie (2006), 'The evolution and allocation of stock options: adapting US-style compensation to the Swedish business model', *European Management Review*, **3** (3), 156–76.

Gompers, Paul, Josh Lerner and David Scharfstein (2005), 'Entrepreneurial spawning: public corporations and the genesis of new ventures, 1986 to 1999', *Journal of Finance*, **60** (2), 577–614.

Hall, Peter and David Soskice (eds) (2001), *Varieties of Capitalism: The Institutional Foundations of Comparative Advantage*, Oxford: Oxford University Press.

Harrison, Bennett (1994), 'The small firms myth', *California Management Review*, **36** (3), 142–58.

Hashemi, Syed M., Sidney Ruth Schuler and Ann P. Riley (1996), 'Rural credit programs and women's empowerment in Bangladesh', *World Development*, **24** (4), 635–53.

Hossain, Farhad (2002), 'Small loans, big claims', *Foreign Policy*, **132**, 79–80, 82.

Hsu, David and Martin Kenney (2005), 'Organizing venture capital: the rise and demise of American research & development, 1946–1973', *Industrial and Corporate Change*, **14** (4), 579–616.

Johnson, Chalmers (1982), *MITI and the Japanese Miracle: The Growth of Industrial Policy, 1925–1975*, Stanford, CA: Stanford University Press.

Kim, Dong-Won and Stuart W. Leslie (1998), 'Winning markets or winning Nobel Prizes? KAIST and the challenges of late industrialization', *Osiris*, 2nd series, **13**, 154–85.

Klepper, Steven (2001), 'Employee startups in high-tech industries', *Industrial and Corporate Change*, **10** (3), 639–74

Koike, Kazuo and Takenori Inoki (eds) (1990), *Skill Formation in Japan and Southeast Asia*, Tokyo: University of Tokyo Press.

Lazonick, William (1983), 'Industrial organization and technological change: the decline of the British cotton industry', *Business History Review*, **57** (2), 195–236.

Lazonick, William (2003), 'Stock options and innovative enterprise: evolution of a mode of high-tech compensation', INSEAD working paper, Fontainebleau, France, August.

Lazonick, William (2005), 'The institutional triad and Japanese development', trans. into Japanese in Glenn Hook and Akira Kudo (eds), *The Contemporary Japanese Enterprise*, Tokyo: Yukikaku Publishing, 55–82.

Lazonick, William (2006a), 'Evolution of the New Economy business model', in Eric Brousseau and Nicola Curien (eds), *Internet and Digital Economics*, Cambridge: Cambridge University Press, pp. 59–113.

Lazonick, William (2006b), 'Globalization of the ICT labour force', in R. Mansell, C. Avgerou, D. Quah and R. Silverstone (eds), *The Oxford Handbook on ICTs*, Oxford: Oxford University Press, pp. 75–99.

Lazonick, William (2007a), 'Innovative enterprise and economic development', University of Massachusetts Lowell Center for Industrial Competitiveness working paper.

Lazonick, William (2007b), 'The US stock market and the governance of innovative enterprise', *Industrial and Corporate Change*, **16** (6), 983–1035.

Lazonick, William (2007c), 'Varieties of capitalism and innovative enterprise', *Comparative Social Research*, **24**, 21–69.

Lazonick, William, Edward March and Öner Tulum (2007), 'Boston's biotech boom: "a new 'Massachusetts Miracle'"?', University of Massachusetts Lowell Center for Industrial Competitiveness, working paper, May, accessed 5 November 2008 at www.uml.edu/centers/CIC.

Lécuyer, Christophe (2006), *Making Silicon Valley: Innovation and the Growth of High Tech, 1930–1970*, Cambridge, MA: MIT Press.

Leslie, Stuart W. (1993a), *The Cold War and American Science: The Military-Industrial Complex at MIT and Stanford*, New York: Columbia University Press.

Leslie, Stuart (1993b), 'How the West was won: the military and the making of Silicon Valley', in William Aspray (ed), *Technological Competitiveness: Contemporary and Historical Perspectives on the Electrical, Electronics, and Computer Industries*, New York: IEEE Press, pp. 75–89.

Leslie, Stuart W. and Robert H. Kargon (1996), 'Selling Silicon Valley: Frederick Terman's model for regional advantage', *Business History Review*, **70** (4), 435–72.

Lu, Qiwen (2000), *China's Leap into the Information Age: Innovation and Organization in the Computer Industry*, New York: Oxford University Press.

Lu, Qiwen and William Lazonick (2001), 'The organization of innovation in a transitional economy: business and government in Chinese electronic publishing', *Research Policy*, **30** (1), 35–54.

Maddison, Angus (2007), 'Historical statistics for the world economy, 1-2003AD', accessed 5 November 2008 at www.ggdc.net/maddison/.

Mallick, Ross (2002), 'Implementing and evaluating microcredit in Bangladesh', *Development in Practice*, **12** (2), 153–63.

Marshall, Alfred (1920), *Principles of Economics*, 8th edn, London: Macmillan.

Mass, William and Andrew Robertson (1996), 'From textiles to automobiles: mechanical and organizational innovation in the Toyoda enterprises, 1895–1933', *Business and Economic History*, **25** (2), 1–37.

Morikawa, Hidemasa (2001), *A History of Top Management in Japan*, New York: Oxford University Press.

National Research Council (1999), *Funding a Revolution: Government Support for Computing Research*, Washington, DC: National Academy Press.

Norberg, Arthur and Judy O'Neill (1996), *Transforming Computer Technology: Information Processing for the Pentagon, 1962–1986*, Baltimore, MD: Johns Hopkins University Press.

Porter, Kelley, Kjersten Bunker Whittington and Walter W. Powell (2005), 'The institutional embeddedness of high-tech regions: relational foundations of the Boston biotech community', in Stefano Breschi and Franco Malerba (eds) *Clusters, Networks, and Innovation*, Oxford: Oxford University Press, pp. 261–96.

Ritter, Jay (2006), 'Some factoids about the 2005 IPO market', University of Florida, accessed 5 November 2008 at http://bear.cba.ufl.edu/ritter.

Saxenian, AnnaLee (2006), *The New Argonauts: Regional Advantage in a Global Economy*, Cambridge, MA: Harvard University Press.

Schumpeter, Joseph A. (1934), *The Theory of Economic Development*, Cambridge, MA: Harvard University Press.

Schumpeter, Joseph A. (1950), *Capitalism, Socialism, and Democracy*, 3rd edn, New York: Harper & Row.

Schumpeter, Joseph A. (1965), 'Economic theory and entrepreneurial history', in Hugh G.J. Aitken (ed.), *Explorations in Enterprise*, Cambridge, MA: Harvard University Press, pp. 45–64.

Shane, Scott (2000), 'Prior knowledge and the discovery of entrepreneurial opportunities', *Organization Science*, **11** (4), 448–69.

Shane, Scott (2003), *A General Theory of Entrepreneurship: The Individual-Opportunity Nexus*, Cheltenham, UK and Northampton, MA, USA: Edward Elgar.

Thornton, Patricia H. (1999), 'The sociology of entrepreneurship', *Annual Review of Sociology*, **25**, 19–46.

United Nations Development Programme (UNDP) (2004), 'Unleashing entrepreneurship: making business work for the poor', Commission on the Private Sector & Development, report to the Secretary-General of the United Nations, UNDP.

Utomi, Pat (2006), 'Why nations are poor', *All Africa*, 7 and 8 February.

Van der Linden, F. Robert (2002), *Airlines and Air Mail: The Post Office and the Birth of the Commercial Aviation Industry*, Lexington, KY: University Press of Kentucky.

Wada, Kazuo (2006), 'The fable of the birth of the Japanese automobile industry: The Toyoda-Platt agreement of 1929', *Business History*, **48** (1), 90–118.

Wahid, Abu N.M. (1994), 'The Grameen Bank and poverty alleviation in Bangladesh: theory, evidence, and limitations', *American Journal of Economics and Sociology*, **53** (1), 1–15.

Whitley, Richard (ed.) (2002), *Competing Capitalisms: Institutions and Economies*, two vols, Cheltenham, UK and Northampton, MA, USA: Edward Elgar.

Woo-Cumings, Meredith (ed.) (1999), *The Developmental State*, Ithaca, NY: Cornell University Press.

World Bank (2004), *Doing Business in 2004: Understanding Regulation*, New York: Oxford University Press.

Xie, Wie and Steven White (2004), 'Sequential learning in a Chinese spin-off: the case of Lenovo Group Ltd.', *R&D Management*, **34** (4) 407–22.

Yonekawa, Shin-ichi (1984), 'University graduates in Japanese enterprises before the second world war', *Business History*, **26** (3), 193–218.

2. The role of public policies in innovation processes

Fabrizio Cobis

INTRODUCTION

The role that governmental policies should play as regards the new and sometimes serious needs of the contemporary economy, which is increasingly 'knowledge-driven', has been deeply questioned in the last few years.

The completely global dimensions of today's economic dynamics force us to consider innovation as the real determining factor on which the competitiveness of a national economic system should be founded.

Such competitive ability appears to be more and more structurally assured by a type of innovation which has its main engine in research, its characterizing element. The ability to produce knowledge, together with the ability to quickly transform that knowledge in economic value, and therefore to rapidly produce high level innovation, represents the key to economic growth and to the competitive success of a country.

Moreover, the strong link between the role of knowledge in innovation and the global characteristics in economic dynamics must be underlined: technological knowledge and economic globalization appear to be mutually enabling factors. The more the economy becomes global, the more innovation plays a fundamental role; an overwhelming technological development yields to wider economic borders, in an endless swirling effect.

THE 'TRIPLE HELIX' MODEL

Within such a context innovative processes, conceptual schemes defining related dynamics, the action and nature of the involved partners, and their relationships are all aspects that have been going through a deep change.

In 1945 Vannevar Bush, scientific advisor of American President Roosevelt, writing his report entitled 'Science, the endless frontier' theorized what in later years would be termed 'the linear model of innovation'. According to Bush, the process of innovation could be represented by a linear sequence, going from the scientific discovery to experimental tests in applied sciences, to subsequent inventions, up to imitative and diffusion processes. Within that model, clear and well-defined areas of competence between basic research, applied research, technological transfer and industrial development can be identified. Consequently, university, private–public research bodies and enterprise areas of action are well outlined.

The conceptual scheme described above has been widely accepted and received wide acclaim in theoretical and empirical studies, up to the 1990s: 'curiosity-driven' or 'mission-oriented' basic research produces results which are then developed and applied through technological and engineering interventions.

Towards the end of the 1990s a different vision has been emerging. Several studies highlight that innovative dynamics is becoming increasingly complex compared to the traditional linear sequence: innovative processes are actually seen to proceed from multiple interactions and interdependences among research, invention, development and production.

The global and widespread character of technological and scientific activities, together with the sharp decrease of a new product time to market, determine the need for a new approach in the design of new innovation dynamics. The classic linear model of innovation is increasingly coupled by an opposite conception, starting from industrial and societal problems to find solutions in science. These two models act together, comprising an interactive model of innovation, where the starting points strengthen one another, and where basic research questions arise from practical problems and vice versa.

Within this picture innovative processes seem increasingly marked by interactive cycles, by circular sequences, where phases and components from various fields are contemporarily involved. An ever-growing cross-fertilization characterizes discipline fields. Researchers and companies tend to be engaged in complementary and integrated research paths.

This new model of innovation implies a deep change in the action and in the role of traditionally prominent figures of the innovative processes: constant and thorough interaction among enterprises, universities and governmental institutions is the key to guarantee competitive growth of a system in a knowledge-based economy.

According to academics (Leydesdorff and Meyer, 2004), the action of these three spheres is pictured as a sort of 'triple helix', where the spheres engage in continuous interactive relations and in complementary actions, one almost playing the role of the other, although not losing their own fundamental mission. In the above scenario Henry Etzkowitz, one of the most important experts of the topic, spoke in 2003 of 'innovation in innovation', meaning that innovation is not only the development of new products, but it should also be the creation of new ways of relating among the three spheres of the triple helix.

THE NEW ROLE OF THE ACTORS INVOLVED IN INNOVATION

According to the new design of innovation processes, the nature and the role of the three subjects involved have been progressively changing. Enterprises become less and less vertically integrated. As stated in an interesting article issued in *The Economist* in March 2007, enterprises increasingly tend to enter networks of external suppliers, going beyond the role of former research divisions. Big US companies obviously still invest a great deal in R&D, but no one seems interested in recreating the huge research labs which once were the main feature of AT&T or Xerox. The boss of Google, Eric Schmidt, considers researchers as 'intellectual mercenaries', supporting the enterprises to solve problems.

Again, *The Economist* (June 2007), describing the reasons for Apple's present renaissance, identifies one of these ingredients as the company's ability to bind together internal ideas with external technologies and solutions, creating increasingly successful products. Companies, in other words, understand that good ideas do not necessarily arise at home: the key to success is networking with public research institutions or with other innovative companies.

The role and nature of university activity itself is changing. Etzkowitz, regarding this aspect, speaks of a second academic revolution: the first added research to traditional teaching activities; now universities are carrying out a new function, that is, to directly contribute to the socio-economic development of societies. Universities and others producing knowledge are increasingly considered as 'generators' of economic growth: they are losing their image of 'ivory towers' to become progressively more entrepreneurial.

According to the above-mentioned model of the 'triple helix', greater importance is given to the ability of universities to interact with enterprises and at the same time to guarantee a proper outcome to research activity results, in terms of new patents and new entrepreneurial initiatives. According to the 'triple helix' model, universities play a fundamental role by raising their action to the level of the other spheres, and supporting their traditional role of knowledge producers with a new role of innovation promoters.

Moreover, the state itself, and more generally government institutions, play a new and more modern role. In the 'triple helix' model, government institutions, at central or regional level, are no longer only in charge of financing other subjects' research activity, granting public funds through selection processes which are not always effective and timely. The state is increasingly playing the role of the actor who establishes the rules of the game and ensures they are actually met, who encourages systemic and deep relations between companies and universities in a wider action aimed at creating better context conditions that are necessary for fostering the growth of the country's innovation capacity.

Within this scenario the state is involved in defining new rules promoting a permanent collaboration between enterprises and universities, support- ing qualified training of research staff, staff mobility from public to private research bodies, promotion of research results, creation of new enterprises from university research activity and diffusion of venture capital activities, while removing potential obstacles at the normative and/or administrative level.

The European Community has partially redesigned its R&D policy to meet this challenge, by issuing the Seventh Framework Programme (2007– 13). Similarly, many countries are now redirecting their public policies on the basis of these new conceptions: typical are the examples of France and Japan in this respect. Italy, though later than others, has acknowledged the need for change: in the past few years public intervention policies, regard- ing the Italian Ministry of Education, University and Research in particu- lar, have been characterized by a new vision, aiming to define new models of intervention rather than simply funding research demand (Figure 2.1).

THE COMMUNITARIAN POLICIES FOR R&D: THE SEVENTH FRAMEWORK PROGRAMME (2007–13)

The reference framework for R&D communitarian policies is the project for a European Research Area (ERA), launched in January 2000 by the European Commission (EC), right before the well-known Lisbon Strategy was started. The ERA is the dimension to apply the actual instruments devoted to promoting R&D. Its aims are clear:

- To break down the frontiers in research.
- To create a common area to best exploit the existing resources.
- To integrate the scientific communities of Eastern and Western Europe.
- To make the 'old country' a place to attract young researchers from all over the world.

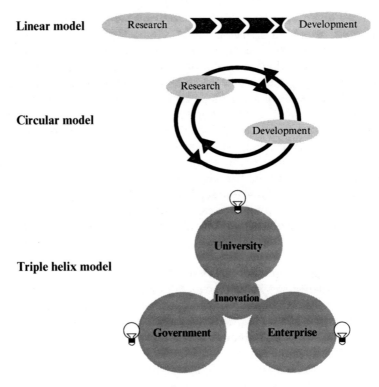

Figure 2.1   The innovation models.

The guidelines issued for these aims to be reached are rational as well as demanding:

- To make the best of material resources and of the infrastructures now existing in Europe.
- To build up a network of excellence.
- To stimulate private investments in research; also to develop effective instruments for protection of intellectual property.
- To create a research system able to fully meet the expectations of civil society about quality of life (for example, environmental protection or personal safety).
- To encourage researchers' mobility; to make research a professional career and attractive for young people; to remove the bureaucratic obstacles hampering the free expression of research.
- To coordinate the EC's research programmes and those of member states in order to avoid future guidelines being issued independently.

In this framework the conclusions of the European Council held in Lisbon on 23–24 March 2000 clearly define the EC's new strategic aim for the decade 2000–10: to make Europe the most dynamic knowledge-based economy in the world. In March 2002 the European Council, held in Barcelona, set a precise goal: to make the European public investments in R&D reach 3 per cent of GDP by 2010, simultaneously raising the private contribution to 2/3 of the total funding.

Seven years later this process was started. It must be pointed out that building the ERA still remains a very challenging aim, considering that nearly 95 per cent of R&D European expenditure is currently decided by member states (in the capital cities), while only 5 per cent is earmarked in Brussels – the common seat – and through a common policy. As a matter of fact, since the Sixth Framework Programme 2000–06 (6FP) establishing a European research area was launched in 2002, action is aimed at R&D joint projects, able to link research teams from different European countries.

One of the strongest points of 6FP was to promote a scheme of planning research based upon common goals, to be pursued only by concentrating all efforts to allow enterprises to overcome concerns from internal competition – a feature that makes particularly strong the research being done in the USA.

In general, it is important to focus on the political road map which has arisen from the Lisbon Strategy in developing the European Council's and the European Commission's programme and communications. First, this strategy suggested a method that has to be applied gradually by member states in working out their policies: the open coordination, aimed at spreading best practices and converging towards the strategic goal; its fundamental passageways are the following:

- By the EC: a coherent definition of its policies, through accurate planning in the short, medium and long term, and by determining qualitative and quantitative indicators and reference parameters in order to measure and compare the performances of each member state.
- By member states: the application of goals and planning criteria, equal for all member states, both at national and regional level.
- To accomplish check and evaluation activities (peer review), aimed at mutual exchange and learning, integrated with monitoring and evaluation schemes performing as a real multilateral supervision system.

In this concrete dimension it was decided to extend the duration of the Framework Programme from four to seven years (Seventh Framework Programme 2007–13), in a logical and temporal connection with the financial perspectives (2007–13); a signal that current EC policy is firmly meant as an essential component of a broader strategy. Also, the new programmes of cohesion policy encourage member states and the regions to invest in systems for supporting innovation (2007–13).

The Seventh Framework Programme (7FP) has been approved in the described context as renewed by the European Council's general guidelines issued in spring 2005 and 2006.

The peculiar aspects of 7FP seem to fit with Lisbon's top priorities:

- simplification of the procedures for participation in the programme;
- implementation of the programme and its budget by theme instead of by instrument, so that it may function more coherently and effectively;
- creation of the European Research Council – with substantial resources – to support exploratory research;
- improved cooperation with industry via the Joint Technology Initiatives (JTI), which will combine private investment and public funding;
- support of a European research infrastructures policy;
- creation of a risk sharing finance facility to make it easier for participants to access European Investment Bank loans.

The innovations in 6FP and 7FP by the EC show that a new public role is emerging: public institutions are less and less simple funding agencies, trying to become proactive actors within the framework by establishing 'game rules', thanks to which the different players (enterprises, universities, research bodies) are able to interact ever more effectively. As hinted at above, the ERA is meant to be the playground where the instruments able to promote R&D may be applied. Also, the skills and expertise being formed through the 6FP's actions in a common – communitarian – dimension should help drive R&D national policies towards a shared vision.

A similar transformation is currently being carried out individually by many countries (both EU and non-EU) in their national public policies of R&D, as the following examples from France, Japan and Italy demonstrate.

EXAMPLES FROM FRANCE AND JAPAN

France

Close to Italy and having a similar standing tradition in promoting territorial policies, recently France has been shown to be particularly active, introducing new measures aimed at stimulating the creation of innovation poles.

In February 2004 DATAR (Délégation à l'aménagement du terri- toire et à l'action régionale – Delegation for land planning and regional policies – significantly renamed at the end of 2005 DIACT, Délégation à l'aménagement et à la compétitivité des territories – Inter-ministerial delegation for territorial planning and competitiveness) presented the new strategies of industrial policy, launching the 'Competitiveness Poles' initia- tive. The *Poles de competitivite* are defined as the combination, in a given local area, of firms, training centres and public or private research units working in partnership to generate synergies around innovative projects.

Attempting to follow the triple helix model, France chose to embrace the Competitiveness Poles formula. This enabled the development of patterns of innovative and shared multiplayer R&D projects from a previous coop- erative/competitive game among players adjusting their roles in a fuzzy fashion. The activities to be carried out in the Competitiveness Poles by its players (companies, research centres, educational institutions) are based upon eight action principles:

1. To identify and to empower the existing poles by labelling them ('labellization').
2. To encourage enterprise networks.
3. To invest in human resources.
4. To create links between industry and research and between industry and education.
5. To facilitate the creation and development of innovative firms.
6. To link poles development with infrastructures (rail, air, land transport).
7. To promote a network policy at the European level.
8. To manage the project with very close participation of regions.

Based on the interventions of the local productive systems model (*Systémes Productifes Locaux*, SPL) in November 2004 the French govern- ment issued a call for proposals (*appel à projet*) open to companies, labo- ratories and research centres, education and training bodies interested in establishing a competitive pole; in particular, the call designated a specific kind of partnership among participants, the legal form of 'association'.

With the support of the state and other public bodies, such as the regions and other bodies for regional development, the above-mentioned players elaborated and submitted their research proposals to the regions. The projects have been evaluated by an inter-ministerial taskforce including delegates of DATAR and the Directorate-General 'Enterprises' established at the Ministry for Economy, Finance and Industry, and comprised also of representatives of the ministries of research, agriculture, defence and labour.

The selection among the 105 submitted projects concerned a threefold analysis: the first, at ministerial level; the second, provided by experts from the business, research and higher education sectors; the third, conducted by regional authorities. On the basis of such a selection, the Inter-ministerial Committee for land planning and development, CIADT (*Comitè Interministerièl d'Amènagement e de Dèveloppement du Territoire*), bestowed the label of 'Competitiveness Poles' to the 66 selected excellence centres during the session held in Paris on 12 July 2005 under the chairmanship of the then Prime Minister De Villepin.

In May 2006 the second call for proposals was closed, and it envisages funding for 68 additional R&D projects submitted by 39 Competitiveness Poles. The two calls allowed support for a total of 165 R&D projects presented by 57 Competitiveness Poles among the 66 so far acknowledged, with 1.5 billion euros earmarked.

The French government identified six internationally acclaimed projects and an additional nine international 'nominees' for their capacity to drive French industry international visibility and for their role played in the global economic competition. A concentration can be identified in the most innovative sectors: ICT, energy, biotech, aeronautical and transportation.

These 15 international clusters, entrusted to a couple of national agencies for their coordination, ANR (for research) and AII (for industrial innovation), pursue six aims:

1. Choose which R&D lines to focus on.
2. Convert poorly competitive firms of the traditional manufacturing sector.
3. Networking the smallest enterprises, so as to overcome the old scheme of industrial districts established on a territorial basis.
4. Arrest the haemorrhage caused by delocalizations.
5. Reduce the technological gap with the most advanced countries.
6. Get fit for winning the 'European Championship' competition that the EU could possibly announce in the near future.

The French initiative of 'Competitiveness Poles' arises from a more general reflection which put the renewal of industrial policies at the centre of governmental strategies. The climax in this reflective process is the well-known report on the state of French industry, written in January 2005 – when the selection of the poles had just been closed – by Saint

Gobain's CEO, Jean Louis Beffa, who also in the past had been adviser to the government playing a very important role in elaborating high-tech programmes under the De Gaulle and Pompidou presidencies (with themes such as nuclear, aerospace, high speed sectors).

In the wake of Laurent Fabius's provocative statement 'If France keeps on like this, it will have only its own name left, written on a sign standing at the entrance of museums', the Beffa Report has shown how in France R&D expenditures are insufficient. It also showed how companies own an average-low technology stock, running the risk of strong competition with the emerging countries (China, India and Eastern Europe).

Beffa's proposal is a renewal in industrial policy based on public promotion of long-term technological programmes, with actions to be taken mainly at the pre-competitive stage (that is, basic research), and furthermore encouraging partnerships between private companies and public administration. In Beffa's opinion, the conversion of the French productive system has to take place turning the 66 selected Competitiveness Poles into the hubs of the whole process, under the coordination of the formerly mentioned AII, Agency for Industrial Innovation, once it has been adequately refinanced.

Japan

According to official statistics, currently Japan turns 3.35 per cent of its GDP into R&D; 79 per cent of it comes from investments by private companies.

The reasons why this country has become a R&D world giant (as the mentioned data seem to suggest) – though it has been devastated as a result of the Second World War aftermaths – are claimed to go back to the industry reorientation, forced just after the conflict: from a research activity primarily oriented to the development of military technologies to one almost exclusively dedicated to the development of consumer goods.

Moreover, the shortage of raw material and the frequent natural disasters (earthquakes, typhoons, volcanic eruptions) urged the country to aim at industry and at R&D processes able to keep products and infrastructures attractive, in terms either of costs (especially in the first post-war phase) or of quality.

Acknowledging the relevant role performed in Japanese society by science and technology (S&T), the parliament in 1995 approved the S&T Basic Law, enacting the country committment to achieve far-reaching goals: to foster the upgrade of industrial products and services; to mitigate the effects of population ageing and of human activities impact on the environment; to cooperate, at an international level, in coping with the globalization process effects. In order to realize projects aiming to attain these goals, Japan conceived a plan with programmes on a four-year basis, named the 'S&T Basic Plan'.

The first S&T Basic Plan was issued in 1996; the second one, dated 2001, has been in force until fiscal year 2005. The application of both plans has determined a deep restructuring of the Japanese R&D system, meant as a reorganization of public research bodies (from state bodies to organizations with independent administration, still under governmental control but taking advantage of a wider autonomy at the managerial level). The Third S&T Basic Plan, in force since 2006 with a 2006–10 total budget of 170 billion euros, aims at raising R&D public support up to 1 per cent of GDP and pursues a reform of the S&T system articulated in a few key points: mobility of human resources and researchers; reform of the public/private collaboration system (patents, licences); promotion of local high-tech districts; reform of the evaluation process; and development of infrastructures.

The actions taken in favour of the sectors considered to be fundamental (life sciences, ICT, environment, nanotechnologies and materials, energy, production technologies, infrastructures, ocean-space frontiers) must mirror S&T's set priority: the internationalization of research. In the second S&T Basic Plan this renewing process was already enforced with the initiative of 'Knowledge Clusters' to be settled on a regional basis through MEXT (Minister of Education, Culture, Sports, Science and Technology), which handles 66 per cent of funds addressed to R&D by the government (15.4 billion euros over a total amount of 23.4 billion euros).

Within a similar strategy to the one adopted almost simultaneously in Italy with the introduction of 'high-tech districts' (I shall elaborate further below), the Japanese Knowledge Cluster is defined as a local technological innovation system organized around universities and other public research institutions with the same R&D themes and potentials; within the region internal and external enterprises are expected to join. All this happens in full respect of the autonomy of local authorities.

It is a system which drives technological innovation through progressive states and creates new enterprises through mutual stimulation between technological seeds in public research institutions and practical needs in the real business world. Such a system tends to generate basic knowledge, according to the triple helix scheme, constituting the core of a continuous technological development process which offers advantages to all actors involved, within global competition.

This initiative benefits from a mixed budget: since 2001 the government has been allocating about €70 million, while regions added about €4 million per year, per cluster. The operative phases of the initiative are the following:

- Identification of 'Knowledge Cluster headquarters' in each region as 'control towers' for project governance.
- Staff including expert coordinators in different fields ('connoisseurs'), with specialized advisors such as patent attorney.
- Realization of industry-academia-government joint research at university research centres or other public institutions, which are expected to produce new technological seeds in accordance with industrial needs.
- Patent registration and development of research results.
- Constant update of research results among system actors through forums.

So far, Japan has launched 18 Knowledge Clusters on the national territory, covering the strategic areas of life sciences, nanotechnologies/materials, environment and mechanics.

The similarities between the actions taken by France (Competitiveness Poles) and Japan (Knowledge Clusters) seem to show that a strong regulatory attempt is being made within the national R&D policies in order to create – in the singular state – a proper scheme for the interactions among the players of innovation.

Italy, as well, in recent years has developed initiatives meant as different ways to approach a new global scheme able to deal with the evolving role of enterprises, universities and research bodies.

THE ITALIAN CASE

In the past decade there has been growing awareness in Italy for the need to support and coordinate policies on scientific and technological research in order to pursue the greater goal of modernizing the country.

Since 1998 the government has been pursuing a deep reorganization of the research sector, in particular through the action of the Ministry of Education, University and Research.

The overall governmental action has been developed according to the triple helix model described above. In recent years, with each reform action, public management showed they well understood and could interpret what the role of the state must be as one of the three helix spheres:

- Support the integration and interaction between public research bodies and enterprises.
- Encourage the establishment of new interactive and circular innovation processes, opposite to the former linear model.

- Sustain the new role which universities could and should play in order to contribute to the socio-economic development of the country.
- Increase enterprises attitude towards an innovative capacity grounded in research.
- Conceive and enact appropriate and efficient rules and environmental conditions.

The Realization of Interventions

The action of the government and in particular of the Ministry of Education, University and Research in order to pursue these objectives has been developed following two main directions, different yet strongly complementary to one another. I refer to strategic and technical actions.

Strategic actions
In April 2002 the Inter-ministerial Committee for Economic Planning (CIPE) approved the new Guidelines for Scientific and Technological Policy of the Italian Government. In so doing, the government defined a precise framework of priorities in order to strengthen already existing areas of excellence; additionally this action aimed at developing excellence in technologically promising areas with higher added value. This framework of priorities for national research has been identified from the following directions:

- The main trends of reference at international level are nowadays represented by three important sectors: information and communications technology (ICT); biotechnology and new materials; nano- and micro-technologies.
- The EC's priorities are: genomics and biotechnologies for health, technology for the information society; nanotechnologies; intelligent materials and new production processes, aeronautics and space; food safety; sustainable development and climate change; governance in a knowledge-based society.
- Evaluation of the impact of investments on the Italian system.

The guidelines identify four strategic axes, completed by cross-sectional interventions:

1. Advancing the frontiers of knowledge, aiming at training new human resources necessary to face the development of the national scientific system and to develop the activity of basic research.
2. Supporting research aimed at developing key enabling cross-sector technologies. The strategic aim of this axis is to realize mission-oriented

research programmes ensuring proper training of young researchers; increasing mobility of researchers among research networks; developing joint public-private laboratories; integrating the national scientific system with the European networks of excellence; developing stronger capacities in the fields with added-value products attractive for the national industrial sector; developing entrepreneurial abilities in the national scientific system (spin-offs).

3. Strengthening industrial research and related technological development, with a view to enhancing the ability of enterprises to turn knowledge and technologies into products services with increased added value. Expected results are: a significant increase of high added-value production; increased qualified occupation in the Italian industrial system; increased propensity of SMEs, especially those located in major industrial areas, to cooperate with the public research system.

4. Promoting the capacity of SMEs to innovate processes and products and to form systemic clusters at the local level. The expected results for this axes are: planning agreements between the state and regions in technologically advanced areas; development of actions in productive fields of specific regional interest through cooperation among universities, public research bodies and SMEs; creation of new entrepreneurship in high-tech fields.

A fifth transversal area of intervention is represented by the strengthening of large infrastructural networks for basic research, mission-oriented research and applied research. Within this axis priority is also given to the increase in internationalization processes of research activities.

Operative actions
Parallel to the advance of the above-mentioned strategic actions, the realization of the governmental research programme has been developed through a series of operative interventions, which are coherent among themselves and functional to the strategic aims.

The main characteristic of all interventions in accordance with the triple helix model has been to write a system of innovative rules enabling the realization of contextual conditions for the competitive enhancement of the entire system. In such a field the following actions must be underlined:

1. Sustain to the creation of new high-tech enterprises, such as public research spin-offs.
2. Realization of joint private–public research labs.
3. Creation and strengthening of high-tech territorial districts.

4. Sustain large research programmes, considered strategic for Italian competitiveness.

All of the interventions have in common the strengthening of the presence and quality of human capital, which constituted a constant objective of ministerial action. The Ministry indeed believes that the necessary de-ageing and qualification processes of Italian researchers can happen within large research projects representing true and proper 'training pipelines'.

Support to the Creation of New High-tech Enterprises, Such as Spin-offs from Public Research

Since 1999 the government has approved Decree n. 297 which represents a true landmark within the support to industrial research activities. Besides reorganizing the already used and well-known grant measures to enterprises, the new normative structure indeed contains absolutely innovative forms of intervention. Among these, it is of particular importance to sustain the new high-tech enterprises, such as spin-offs. For the first time, there is the possibility that public research actors can pursue their own activities through the realization of new entrepreneurial initiatives.

In this framework a key role is played by venture capitalists who can offer new opportunities (not available up to now) and a direct engagement in supporting innovative ideas. This constitutes one of the most significant innovations deriving from the reform of the industrial research system in Italy. The Ministry intends to aid the creation of new highly technological enterprises as a result of start-up processes from public research. Otherwise stated, the Ministry supports those professors, researchers and public research bodies willing and able to transform a suitable research project into a potentially successful entrepreneurial initiative.

Inspired by a similar intervention of the French system, the decree enables university professors and researchers, researchers of public bodies, or PhD students and research fellows to apply for funding to the Ministry with classic research projects, to be carried out in collaboration with their university or with other companies and venture capital investors. Applicants must commit to creating a new company within three months since the selection of the project held by the Ministry.

The Ministry evaluates such projects through a special commission which has the responsibility not only to ensure that qualitative scientific and technical requirements are met, but also to assess the project's potential in terms of new business for the constituting company. Particular attention is paid to the financial and business plan that applicants must submit for the new company, and to any other aspect concerning such a project.

Table 2.1   The 2001–8 spin-offs promoted by MIUR

	2001	2002	2003	2004	2005	2006	2007	2008	TOTAL
SUBMITTED PROPOSALS	18	23	8	14	28	16	13	3	123
APPROVED PROPOSALS	5	5	3	7	17	11	7		55
APPROVED COSTS (million euros)	3.5	5.5	2.6	6.7	14.4	8.2	4.3		45.5
MIUR CONTRIBUTION (million euros)	2.0	1.9	1.3	3.1	7.4	4.6	2.2		22.8

Among these aspects, a competitive edge is given to those initiatives which include venture capital firms: the Ministry assigns great importance to these providers in the process of start-up support, also considering their role in many successful high-tech initiatives, especially in the USA. The ministerial support is given in the form of free grants, according to European limitations, and for a maximum of 500 000 euros for each project.

Table 2.1 and Figure 2.2 show the figures and the facts related to the spin-off initiative, updated to 2008.

Realization of joint public-private research labs

The regulations contained in Decree n. 297/99 additionally enabled the realization of another crucial initiative in Southern Italy, that is, the con-stitution of the so called 'joint labs', or public-private laboratories.

With such a move, the Ministry intended to promote the realization and/or the strengthening of strong scientific and technological competency clusters in specific strategic sectors with highly innovative potential. Such clusters are characterized by an ongoing collaboration between industrial enterprises and public research bodies. These concentrations are defined as 'laboratories'.

This measure was included within the wider framework designed by the Guidelines for Science and Technology Policy, approved by CIPE in 2002. Among its priorities, CIPE identified the need for a decisive redefinition of the science and technology strategy of public support for innovation in Southern Italy, based on the collaboration between public and private scientific bodies, in sectors where the quality of human resources is vital.

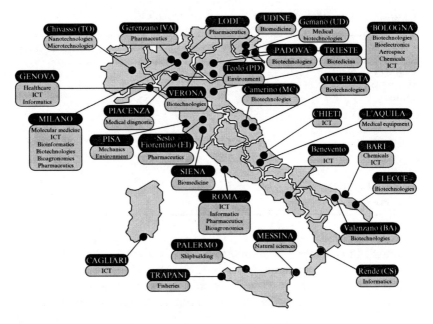

Figure 2.2   Map of the spin-offs promoted by MIUR.

The shift was thus aimed at accompanying the convergence of measures for Southern Italy in technological sectors and areas enabling the growth of a sustainable Italian competitiveness. This has been translated into two types of measures, sustaining:

1. Research finalized at the modernization of the manufacturing and other advanced sectors, already based in Southern Italy;
2. The growth of new high-tech economic activities in sectors such as biomedicine, biotechnology, new drugs, food and agriculture, micro-mechanics and transport. Subsidies have also been foreseen for ICT platforms primarily applied to the development of new products, and to tourism, food and agriculture, and e-learning.

With a budget of €240 million, the realized interventions also aimed at enhancing, consolidating and integrating R&D investments already placed by the Ministry through its funds (Basic Research Fund, Industrial Research Fund, National Operative Plan in underdeveloped areas), which enabled the emergence and selection of successful public-private research entities. Within this framework projects have been selected based on their ability to:

- Sustain modernization processes and the growth of high-tech enterprises in the Southern Italian production system.
- Consolidate and foster the settlement of R&D and designing activities, deriving from national and multinational companies and public research bodies.
- Accelerate internationalization processes of the Southern Italian scientific and technologic system.
- Enable the participation of young researchers in projects with potential innovative market applications.

The Ministry pursued these objectives through subsidies granted to specific projects integrating industrial and pre-competitive research with high-level training of qualified personnel. The selection and financing process has been carried out according to Article 12 of Ministerial Decree no. 593 issued on 8 August 2000, and subsequent modifications and integrations. This decree enacts regulations foreseen by Decree no. 297/99. The selected projects share the characteristic of being developed within the above-mentioned laboratories, enabling their stabilization over the medium to long term.

Within this setting laboratories are thus designed as organization units characterized by the following distinctive elements:

- Concentration of activities at one site, with multidisciplinary competencies and multipurpose scientific instruments, and high innovative potential.
- Integration, within the same site, of public research structures and industrial enterprises.
- Organization and management structure.
- Capacity to develop industrial, pre-competitive research and training activities in an integrated manner and in the medium to long term.
- Capacity to enhance research results, also in terms of trademarks, registered trademarks and industrial start-ups.
- Presence of a network of scientific and industrial collaborations, external to the laboratory, also on an international basis.

The technological areas of intervention are the following:

1. Development of innovative technologies for advanced medical diagnosis.
2. Development of technologies for thermal solar energy at high temperature.
3. Development of innovative technologies for advanced production systems.

4. Development of e-business platforms enabling innovative applications in the food and agriculture sector, in tourism, in cultural heritage and in the development of new products.
5. Development of innovative biotechnological platforms for the identification of new anti-infective drugs.
6. Economically interesting genomics applied to the improvement and to the certification of specific vegetable species (tomatoes, wheat, grape).
7. Development of polymeric materials applied to electronics for the realization of new chips.
8. Bioinformatics applied to genomics.
9. Development of technologies for the realization of new materials and development of design methods for the train sector and for medium-size vectors. Realization of facilities for tests and qualification.
10. Development of technologies and platforms for controlled studies aimed at the assessment of pharmaceutical efficacy on animals and humans.
11. Resources finalized at open-source software.

In such areas 26 projects have been funded, rounding up to in excess of €210 million.

Creation and Strenghtening of High-tech Territorial Districts

It must be underlined that Decree no. 297/99 enabled highly innovative measures with the joint participation of the Ministry and local authorities. Through actions identified and coordinated within specific programme agreements, it has been possible to realize and sustain high-tech districts which represent a true innovation in territorial development policy. Such agreements represent a new development model involving the partnership of enterprises and scientific bodies (universities and other public research entities), in addition to public and private financial institutions and local authorities, all operating within a unitary and strategic design.

Long after the Second World War the Italian system was believed to justify its competitiveness also – and sometimes mostly – on the vitality of enterprises located within industrial districts and on their high vocation for exports. These enterprises could actually count on their flexibility, tactics and strategic rapid action, local networking and collaboration with other enterprises, light bureaucracy and slim organization. Actually, the performance of such enterprise systems has been of undisputed relevance and marked particularly positive periods of the Italian industrial system evolution. More recently, the bulk of district enterprises complemented and in many cases fortunately subsidized the large enterprise, since the latter has shown its vulnerability (generally, in competitiveness and, specifically, in maintaining occupation) firstly in Southern Italy, and subsequently in the rest of the country.

The district model has been and still is identified as an example of Italian best practice, which might be of interest for many countries: for developed countries it was a model for the consolidation of the industrial base supporting large enterprises; for the developing countries the Italian district was a recipe to initiate economic development through a bottom-up approach, with low infrastructural investments and low entry barriers, full exploitation of low-cost labour and with a good impact on employment rates.

Nonetheless, it is acknowledged that today the competitiveness of Italian districts is seriously threatened, or at least under careful reconsideration. It appears urgent to reflect upon and discuss political actions aimed at enhancing the positive aspects of the district economy, which should be defended and further expanded. District competitiveness is particularly threatened in a sort of 'pincer manoeuvre' by:

- Fierce competition from large international/multinational companies, basing their product development and marketing strategies on high R&D investments and on exceptionally wide distribution channels, representing insurmountable entry barriers to many district systems.
- The emergence of competitors from developing countries, with mass production of good quality at low costs that are out of reach for Italian enterprises. Such countries possess sufficient technological know-how and substantial advantages in terms cost factors.

Technological districts are defined as territorial aggregations of high-tech activities, true and proper innovation hubs where public research bodies, large enterprises, new or existing small enterprises and local authorities make their contribution. At present, technological districts represent an extremely promising potential in Italy, given two factors: (1) the consolidation and decline of scientific parks; (2) the new dynamism expressed by universities and by a few large enterprises in recent years, emerging as true managers of territorial development. From this point of view, technological districts enhance the necessity to develop composite innovation processes, enriched by the contribution of various subjects with different competencies and aims. Also, international experiences exist to refer to for technological districts. However, Italian characteristics cannot be ignored, as they could constitute a lever for growth processes in the future.

The first feature is Italian attractiveness as a site for R&D centres of multinational companies, given the quality and relative convenience of Italian graduates. From this point of view, Italy represents an alternative, obviously with different characteristics, to the localization of R&D laboratories in emerging countries such as India.

The second Italian feature is the variety of technological districts. Notwithstanding a rigid definition, metropolitan areas where many high-tech public and private activities are located are sometimes defined as technological districts, such as Milan or Rome.

A slightly different situation owe the technological districts based in Turin, where the characterizing element is the presence of a limited number of large private research laboratories (like Telecom Italia Lab – TIlab and Centro Ricerche Fiat – CRF), which typify the district. In other non-metropolitan areas, not only is the number of researchers high in absolute terms, but its incidence in that area is much higher than the national penetration. This is the case of Pisa, where several high-tech enterprises have been created close to university and Consiglio Nazionale delle Recerche [National Council of Research] (CNR) premises.

The most relevant priority for a policy addressing technological districts in Italy is to accelerate the collaboration between private and public institutions backed by institutional agreements among central administrations, regions and local authorities. These considerations motivated the interventions of the Ministry in such an important sector. The aim is to promote and stimulate a competitive process among the regions for the creation of internationally acclaimed research and innovation poles of excellence in numerous Italian areas. The ultimate goal is to accelerate the technology transfer process within agreed projects among the various actors of the scientific and innovation system in Italy.

Technological districts: characteristics, requirements, operative procedures: how MUR acts like a provider of funds and rules

The realization of a technological district is based upon the existence of a few essential elements which represent a pre-condition for growth and development. One of the fundamental concepts of districts policy, as it results from the analysis of the rules fixed for their creation, is represented by the valorization of a specific local identity.

Therefore an endogenous development is realized, generated by the accumulation of specific competencies, increasing the capacity to attract external stakeholders (such as entrepreneurs, multinational companies and research centres) and thus global competencies and knowledge.

Basic conditions for a territory to attract external investments are:

- widespread entrepreneurship
- highly qualified human resources
- presence of renowned universities
- support of an adequate network of infrastructures
- availability of technological transfer services
- high standards of living.

The process to be carried out is not straightforward as it involves a series of actors that are different in nature and mission: companies and research bodies (public and private), each of them interested in participating in a common strategy, able to increase competition in a given area, and also to stand out internationally. The common commitment should be to create a system where research and entrepreneurial activities, the development of existing activities and the availability of capital investments are all linked together and 'self-feeding'.

A project where the main objective is the creation of a technological district begins with an assessment of the existing conditions. The region is promoting the territorial analysis, committing to the constitution of a negotiation table with all interested partners (entrepreneurs' associations, for example), with the aim to build awareness of the project at local level.

In order to launch actions generating a district, it is fundamental to examine the entrepreneurial structure of a particular sector. In order to do so, workshops and seminars addressed to all actors involved are a potential solution, aiming at describing the identified industrial environment, and indicating steps to be taken for the creation of an efficient system of services and connections which can be useful to companies wishing to attract new investments.

Once the potential and availability of a territory to develop a challenging development in a given sector has been analysed, the region drafts a proposal to be sent to the MIUR, which assesses its feasibility. The assessment of initial conditions is carried out in collaboration with a state agency called Sviluppo Italia.

Once the initial situation is outlined in the studies supplied by the region and in the analyses carried out by the Ministry and Sviluppo Italia, it is possible to define the agreements that allow the district to be operative. A so-called Agreement Protocol (*Protocollo di intesa*) can often be previously signed by the Minister and the President of the region, right before the Plan Agreement (*Accordo di Programma*). The *Protocollo d'intesa* aims at the creation of the district: it is a political document signed by the parties engaging in the realization of district objectives. The Plan Agreement is a technical document which aims at stating the activities of the various subjects involved. Some Plan Agreements can be signed by the Ministry of Economy and Finance (MEF) too. This happens when MEF supplies specific resources to the MIUR or the region. In this case, the agreement is called the Framework Plan Agreement (*Accordo di Programma quadro*).

The agreement is therefore subscribed by different party enterprises, private and public research bodies and the national and local government. Once the agreement is signed, a strong structure of governance is needed in order to coordinate the district. Its aim is to support research activities and accelerate start-up processes and development, through a strategy shared by the main actors in the area. According to the Plan Agreement, every actor plays a different role which are described below. The Ministry is engaged in:

- Participating in the organization and control of the action.
- Financing the initiatives of excellence as regards research and higher education, based on projects and according to concrete and measurable objectives.
- Financing initiatives aimed at accelerating the economic impact of ideas, based on projects and according to concrete and measurable objectives.
- Financing initiatives aimed at creating R&D centres of excellence and at enhancing research results to promote new entrepreneurial activities.

The Ministry funds the district according to the dimension of the initiative itself. It is important to underline that MIUR uses resources which are the usual instruments of its institutional activity; among these the most used resources of funding are those presented in the Decree 297/99, or 'Reorder of the law and procedures to support scientific and technological research, to spread technology and increase mobility of researchers'.

A member of the board of management of the district usually comes from the Ministry. Besides the participation of the government, there are local bodies too: regions, Town Halls (Comuni), provinces and various associations, each one having the right to nominate a member of the board and funding the initiatives. The region, in particular, like the Ministry, uses its own funding tools to improve infrastructures, logistics and training, and to hire highly qualified human resources and so on.

Universities and research bodies are not obliged to fund the initiatives of the district. They may take part in organizing, in monitoring the district and, according to its aims, in addressing part of their research activities; they may also promote initiatives to enhance entrepreneurship.

Universities can make their resources available to the district and contribute to the valorization of intellectual property of their researchers.

The organization of the district is usually entrusted to a body constituted with this purpose. This body usually connects research, the input, with the output, which can be a patent, a start-up or a spin-off project. In order to promote the activities of the district, the coordinating body carries out any initiative possibly useful to develop strategies able both to strengthen research activities in the field of the district and to accelerate the creation and growth of entrepreneurial activities in the same field.

At present, 25 technological districts have been launched: Figure 2.3 shows their nationwide distribution, and their specific technological characters. For each district, the Ministry granted public resources, essentially coming from the FAR (*Fondo per le Agevolazioni alla Ricerca*, Research Aids Fund), deriving from Decree 297/99, for a total of €300 million.

Support to Large Strategic Research Programmes for the Competitiveness of the Country

The 2005–07 National Research Programme (NRP), approved by CIPE in its session of 18 March 2005, indicated the launch of 12 strategic programmes among its main intervention in favour of the competitive capacity of Italy's industrial system:

1. Public health (study and treatment of cancers and degenerative diseases with new approaches derived from human genome knowledge).
2. Revitalization of the pharmaceutical industry through fine chemistry of natural compounds for new diagnostic applications and new active molecules.
3. New applications for the biomedical industry.
4. Advanced systems of manufacturing with impact not only on machine tools, but also on manufacturing sectors typically 'made in Italy', such as textiles, apparel and tool mechanics.
5. Development and strengthening of the motor industry, including motorbikes with low consumption motors and low environmental impact.
6. Ship building, aeronautics and helicopter building with high penetration in foreign markets.
7. Advanced materials (particularly ceramics) for structural applications.
8. Innovative broad-band telecommunications systems with the use of satellites for different applications in security, prevention and intervention in cases of natural disasters.

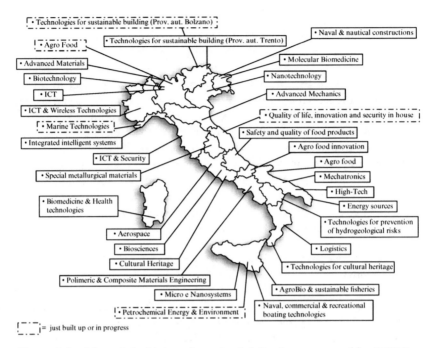

Figure 2.3   Map of the high-tech territorial districts promoted by MIUR.

9.   Valorization of typical food agricultural products and food security through new characterization systems and quality guarantees.
10. Transports and advanced logistics, info-mobility of people and goods.
11. ICT and electronic components.
12. Energy saving and distributed microgeneration.

These strategic programmes have been conceived as an integrated and organized set of basic research actions, industrial research, pre-competitive development and training of excellent human capital which, reciprocally nourishing, can pursue the parallel objectives both in the short term (especially through activities of industrial research and pre-competitive development) and in the long run (through basic research).

In such a view the strategic programmes had to include actions with the joint participation of enterprises, universities, public research bodies and any other public or private actor in research and innovation; all this with the aim of creating conditions for the realization of organized and structural collaboration platforms between enterprises and the public research system. By identifying such programmes, the government has thus recognized the role of research as a strategic factor for the improvement of Italian competitiveness, with interventions that are fully coherent with the triple helix model.

Enterprises, universities and public research bodies overwhelmingly responded to the invitation of the Ministry: over an initial availability of €1100 million, 740 project ideas have been submitted and, out of these, the best ones have been transformed into over 150 executive projects distributed in the above-mentioned programmes. At present, these activities are in their full developmental phase.

What seems to emerge from this survey of MIUR actions is the change in MIUR's R&D policy. Having to cope with an ever evolving meaning of innovation (the triple helix is only one of the latest models), the Ministry progressively changed the way to support enterprises in making R&D activities: from a widespread and indistinct funding process, which did not take into account what is peculiar in each region and of the territorial various academic specializiations, to a systemic action of analysis, planning, rule making and selected funding.

The MIUR today sees its role as guidance for everyone in Italy involved in R&D: its real task is to build a sort of 'road map', made of different trails (the illustrated initiatives), each of them leading to the ultimate goal, the competitive enhancement of the whole system.

Keeping in mind the objective set by the Lisbon Strategy (to make Europe the strongest knowledge-based economy in the world by 2010), MIUR will keep on creating the necessary coordination among enterprises, universities and research bodies, aiming at the increase of financial support to research from the private sector.

This could imply MIUR revises some specific aspects of the initiatives taken: for example, the governance system of each techological district probably has to be reconsidered in order to strengthen its independence. But the best practices born in the overall process are a starting point for the development of the future strategies, even beyond 2010.

ACKNOWLEDGEMENTS

The author gratefully acknowledges the valuable contribution of Dott. Alessandro Ricci for the realization of this work

BIBLIOGRAPHY

Barcelona European Council (2002), *Presidency Conclusions*, SN 100/4/2/ REV1, 15 and 16 March.

Beffa, Jean Louis (2005), 'Renewing industrial policy', accessed at www.planotec-nologico.pt/document/rapport_jean_louis_beffa.pdf 15 January.

Bush, Vannevar (1945), 'Science – the endless frontier', Washington DC, US Government Printing Office, accessed May 2007 at www.nsf.gov/od/lpa/nsf50/vbush1945.htm#ch1.

Council of the European Union (2006), 'Council approves EU research programmes for 2007–2013', (press release 336) 16887/06.

Council of the European Union (2002), 'Structuring the European Research Area, 2002–2006', decision 2002/835/EC of 30 September 2002 adopting a specific programme for research, technological development and demonstration.

Etzkowitz Henry (2003), 'Innovation in innovation: The triple helix of university-industry-government Relations', *Social Science Information*, **42** (3), 293–338.

European Parliament and Council of the European Union (2002), decision 1513/2002/EC of 27 June 2002 concerning the sixth framework programme of the European Community for research, technological development and demonstration activities, contributing to the creation of the European Research Area and to innovation, 2002–2006.

Interministerial Committee for Economic Planning – CIPE (Comitato Interministeriale per la Programmazione Economica) (2002), *Scientific Guidelines for Scientific and Technological Policy of the Italian Government*, accessed May 2007 at www.miur.it/0003Ricerc/0141Temi/0478PNR_-_/1886PNR_-_.htm.

Italian Ministry of Education, University and Research (2007), *National Research Programme 2005–2007* – PON (Programma Nazionale di Ricerca), accessed May 2007 at www.miur.it/0003Ricerc/0141Temi/0478PNR_-_/1886PNR_-_.htm.

Leydesdorff Loet and Martin Meyer (2004), 'The triple helix of university-industry-government relations', *Scientometrics*, **58** (2), 191–2003.

Lisbon European Council (2000), *Presidency Conclusions*, accessed at www.europarl.europa.eu/summits/lis1_en.htm, 23 and 24 March.

The Economist (2007), 'The rise and fall of corporate R&D. Out of the dusty labs', March.

The Economist, (2007), 'Lessons from Apple. What other companies can learn from California's master of innovation', 9 June.

3. Finding, financing and growing technology-based innovations: a perspective on MIT

David Verrill

INTRODUCTION

Schumpeter's vision in 1939 about entrepreneurial innovation as a key driver of the economy is even more true today, as creative destruction is exhibited in a new technology-driven economy. In 2007 US venture capital companies invested nearly $30 billion in technology ventures – more than half of them in California (Silicon Valley) and Massachusetts (Boston/Cambridge). Individual, wealthy 'angel' investors contributed nearly the same amount ($26 billion) of capital, investing largely in early stage companies.

Universities like the Massachusetts Institute of Technology (MIT) act as important engines of innovation. In 2007 MIT sponsored more than $600 million of research. A good portion of that was funnelled through interdisciplinary research centers that bring expertise from different schools and departments together to solve complex problems. A BankBoston study (Ayers, 1997) performed in 1997 showed that MIT had spawned more than 4000 companies which employed more than a million people and had revenues of nearly $250 billion a year – or the equivalent in 1997 of the 24th largest economy in the world above South Africa, Greece and Norway.

The Boston/Cambridge area has a key set of ingredients that make it a dynamic ecosystem of innovation. These ingredients are similar to other parts of the USA that are also sources of innovation – Silicon Valley and Orange County in California, Research Triangle in North Carolina and Austin in Texas.

MIT's role in enabling innovation is undeniable. But in addition to MIT, the Boston/Cambridge area provides a critical set of ingredients that allow the region to be a key driver of innovation in the US economy.

This chapter provides a brief view into this technology-driven, innovation marketplace in the USA with a focus on MIT's role as a driver of innovation.

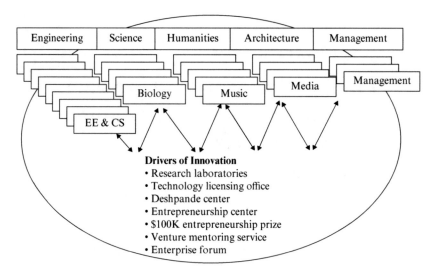

Figure 3.1   MIT's ecosystem of innovation.

UNIVERSITIES AS ENGINES OF INNOVATION

While MIT is a modestly sized university with about 10 000 students, there are some telling statistics that indicate its focus on research and innovation.

- About 60 per cent of the students are enrolled in graduate programs.
- Currently there are about 1000 teaching faculty, but there are also about 2000 researchers working within a 'dual ladder' system.
- In 2007 more than $1 billion of the overall operating budget at MIT was dedicated to sponsored research – a staggering 45.3 per cent.
- In 2007 about $75 million in research was provided from corporations.
- There are approximately 100 interdisciplinary research labs and centers.

Figure 3.1 depicts one view of the MIT ecosystem of innovation. Like many universities, MIT has 'schools' with 'departments' of specific courses of study. What makes MIT unique is a 60-year heritage of interdisciplinary research labs and centers where faculty, research staff, students, government agencies and corporations work collectively on a huge variety of subjects, ranging from the Media Lab, to the Materials Science Consortium, to the Center for Digital Business, to the Computer Science and AI Lab, to the Microfabrication Center.

Entrepreneurials themselves, individual faculty and researchers have started these centers at their own initiative. The president of MIT does not strategically decide that any of these labs should exist. Quite the contrary. A single faculty member or researcher generates the seed of an idea, propagates that idea to peers and develops a plan to launch a larger, collective effort. With the permission of the appropriate school dean – the owner of faculty time and their physical space – the group is formed with outreach to sources of funding, using a standard set of agreements managed centrally by MIT. Often a professional manager will be hired, as will staff, depending upon the scale of the activity. And while each group reports to a specific department or dean, the faculty, students and researchers can be drawn from any school or any department, regardless of affiliation. The underlying notion is that today's complex problems require a multi-disciplinary approach to solve them. Labs and centers are thus able to avoid the inevitable 'silos' that can often stymie good research. All of these labs and centers were started in this manner, and they survive based upon their own merit.

Because many of these centers take advantage of corporate support, there is an acknowledged effort to shorten the distance between long-term academic research and short-term corporate interests. This 'line in the sand' is something that MIT has done an excellent job of managing for more than half a century – maintaining all the proprieties of academic necessity, while serving the interests of industry. This heritage of working closely with industry (and the US Federal Government) is usually attributed to the necessities brought on by World War II. As a nation – with government support as well as corporate support – the emphasis on technological advantage as a tipping point in the war became a rallying point at universities like MIT. Radar, for example, was invented and developed at the MIT 'Rad Lab' and many consider it to be one of the technological advantages that led to the US triumph in the war. After 60 years of practicing this collaborative effort, it is a part of the 'DNA' of MIT. But even before that, all the way back to its founding in 1861 – MIT has focused on both the 'mind and the hand'. Thinking and doing, together. 'Mens et manus' is the founding motto of MIT.

Yet the mere existence of these many labs and centers is only half the story. The other half of the story revolves around the myriad number of mechanisms for the transfer of results of the research into meaningful enterprises. Below is a brief discussion of a few of these mechanisms.

Industrial Liaison Program

For more than 60 years the MIT Industrial Liaison Program (ILP) has facilitated connections between more than 200 member companies and the faculty and research staff of MIT. Two dozen industrial liaison officers (ILOs) streamline access to MIT through meetings and events that match the interest of personnel from member companies. Companies pay an annual fee (typically $50 000 to $75 000) for these connection services, and have unlimited access to the campus. ILOs are often alumni of MIT, and have decades of work experience that allows them to easily bridge the gap between commercial interests and technical innovation at MIT. A typical ILO will have a specific knowledge base which is matched with the general interests of a small portfolio of corporate members. The ILO acts as the 'eyes and ears' on campus to help companies connect with the right people, build meaningful relationships with them and facilitate more formal relationships.

Member companies use the ILP to keep pace with the latest in technology and innovation, find specific areas of research to invest in more deeply and potentially attract graduating students to join their company. Faculty and research staff on campus that meet with ILP members participate in a 'revenue sharing' program such that fees that the ILP takes in are distributed annually to faculty and research staff who meet with member companies. A recent article in the *Sloan Management Review* offers a useful perspective on why and how companies connect to MIT through the ILP (Wright, 2008) (http://ilp-www.mit.edu/).

Technology Licensing Office

MIT's Technology Licensing Office (TLO) manages all the intellectual property (IP) generated at the Institute – regardless of the source of support for that research.[1] In 2007 more than 500 'Disclosures of Invention' were filed through the TLO, with more than 300 patent filings as a result. More than 100 patents were granted to MIT through the TLO in 2007.

More than 20 companies were launched from licensed MIT technology in 2007. In terms of revenue, 600 active licenses generated gross revenues of nearly $50 million. Through revenue sharing and inventors departments and the Institute share net revenues in roughly equal parts. The TLO is a very professionally managed organization, with very streamlined processes for identifying IP and protecting it through patents. It is also very good at making this IP available to corporations, venture capitalists and entrepreneurs alike through a reasonable set of licensing terms. The system is optimized at every angle – making the IP easily accessible, and rewarding each of the players (internally and externally to MIT) based upon the ultimate commercial success of the IP. This attitude of both protecting and promoting the IP is essential to the overall ecosystem of innovation at MIT – and a relatively significant contributor to the Institute's budget (http://web.mit.edu/tlo/www/).

Deshpande Center

Founded in 2002 with a generous gift from entrepreneur Desh Deshpande – Founder/CEO of Sycamore Networks – the Deshpande Center provides approximately $1 million per year to a dozen or more MIT-based research teams that are working on ideas with commercial promise. Since its founding, more than 75 projects have received grants of nearly $9 million. There are two types of grants – ignition and innovation. Ignition grants are in support of 'proof of concept' activities, while innovation grants are for validation activities.

Of those groups receiving grants, 14 have spun out of MIT as independent companies that have thus far raised more than $100 million in venture capital. These grants act as an important source of capital to prove and develop novel concepts discovered in the labs on campus, particularly from younger faculty. Only MIT people can receive the grants, which are provided as gifts that provide no ownership to the Deshpande Center or MIT. While the Deshpande Center is located in the School of Engineering, any MIT faculty can apply and receive grants (http://web.mit.edu/deshpandecenter/).

Entrepreneurship Center

One of the oldest and largest educational programs focused on innovation and entrepreneurship is the MIT Entrepreneurship Center at the MIT Sloan School of Management. The Entrepreneurship Center's website describes how they 'educate the men and women who make high tech start-up companies successful'. Entrepreneurship is a 'concentration' option within the MBA curriculum, with a variety of courses geared towards training entrepreneurs. These courses are also open to cross-registrants from any of the other schools on campus. Through courses, contests, events and other networking exercises, students are introduced to all the necessary resources to support their current and future entrepreneurial activities. The center has also helped set up other entrepreneurship centers across the globe, in the UK, Taiwan and Dubai (http://entrepreneurship.mit.edu/).

MIT $100K Entrepreneurship Competition
The $100K competition was founded in 1990 and has become one of the premier business plan competitions in the USA. Students and researchers

in the MIT community are invited to present their plans in a year-long competition with multiple phases. The whole effort is entirely managed by MIT students who raise money from sponsors (typically law firms, venture capitalists and consulting firms), coordinate expert judges, match entrants with venture mentors and execute a competition typically with more than 200 entrants. Each three to five-member team must have at least one MIT student on the team, although many teams have students from other universities. Areas of focus for the 2008 competition include aero/astro, biotech, development, energy, mobile, product/services and web/IT. Winners in each category move to the finals, where the top four teams receive cash awards to help start their companies. There are more than 100 successful startups that have resulted from this competition. The 2007 winners were Robopsy (robotic assistant to radiologists), Bagazo (cooking fuel from biological waste), C3 Bioenergy (unique methods for new biofuels) and Promethean Power (solar turbine) (www.mit100k.org).

Venture Mentoring Service
The Venture Mentoring Service (VMS) was launched in 2000 to provide mentoring, help and advice to any MIT student, faculty, alumni or member of staff who is in the process of starting a company. The volunteer mentors are very accomplished executives from a variety of disciplines, successful entrepreneurs from many sectors and experienced faculty who have successfully started companies from their own labs. There is no cost for the service. Mentors are matched with entrepreneurs based upon several criteria which ensure industry sector, technology and/or functional complements. Mentors often spend a tremendous amount of time over a number of years to help companies grow in the marketplace. There are now several hundred mentors actively involved in the VMS (http://web.mit.edu/vms).

Enterprise Forum
The Enterprise Forum was founded in 1978 and acts as a resource to anyone in business who would like to promote and strengthen the success of their technology-oriented company. With 18 chapters in the USA and six countries, regular meetings involve company presentations to an expert panel of reviewers and an audience of entrepreneurs, venture capitalists, angels, lawyers, accountants and potential employees who critique and advise the company. The Enterprise Forum itself is a not-for-profit company (http://enterpriseforum.mit.edu).

External connection points
Each of the activities noted above is geared toward removing any friction of movement for innovation in the various labs and centers at MIT toward

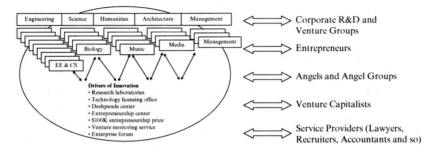

Figure 3.2   MIT's connection points for commercialization of innovation.

commercialization. All would be for naught unless there were a variety of players who can translate innovation into commercial enterprises. Again, the Boston area is a unique ecosystem of universities, corporate R&D and venture groups, entrepreneurs, functional professionals, angels and angel groups, venture capitalists and service providers, such as lawyers, recruiters, accountants, real estate managers and so on (Figure 3.2). There are literally hundreds of each of these providers laying in wait for the next big idea that they can develop, commercialize and financially benefit from. Six of the top eight pharmaceutical companies in the world have offices on the edge of the MIT campus to encourage a flow on people, information and knowledge. Google and Microsoft have opened significant research centers, again, on the edge of campus, to take full advantage of proximity to MIT. There are more than 50 venture capital firms within a 30-minute drive of campus.

ECONOMIC IMPACT OF MIT AND OTHER UNIVERSITIES IN THE BOSTON AREA

In 1997 BankBoston sponsored an exhaustive study to determine how MIT technology and alumni have contributed to the economy in terms of revenues and employment. At the time, more than 4000 US-based and MIT founded companies were studied. Collectively, their revenues were about $232 billion in 1997. The companies alone constituted the equivalent of the 24th largest economy in the world – above South Africa, Greece and Norway. The companies employed some 1.1 million people and were largely concentrated in California, Massachusetts, Texas, New Jersey and Pennsylvania. Approximately 80 per cent were manufacturing based.

Outside of the USA the numbers were similarly impressive. More than 200 MIT founded companies in Europe (67), Latin America (52), Asia (31), Canada (20), East Asia (19) and the Middle East (12) were listed, with about 65 per cent of them consulting companies versus manufacturing (35 per cent).

MIT is not the only research university in Boston, where there are in fact eight major research universities including Boston College, Boston University, Brandeis, Harvard, MIT, Northeastern, Tufts and the University of Massachusetts. Collectively they conducted more than $1.5 billion in research in the year 2000. They also purchased $1.3 billion of goods and services from local providers, and spent more than $1 billion on construction projects. These eight universities employed more than 51 000 people in 2000, and more than 310 000 of their alumni living in the greater Boston area.

The Venture Community

In 2007 the US venture capital community raised $35 billion in new funds, and invested nearly $26 billion from existing funds in US companies. Individual 'angel' investors invested nearly the same amount, mostly in early stage companies. In fact, more than 235 000 angels and 200 angel groups funded more than 51 000 companies, while Venture Capitalists (VCs) funded just less than 4000 companies. These are huge numbers, and point out a couple of interesting trends. First, angel investors are investing roughly the same amount of capital in more than ten times as many companies, with a preference for early stage companies. VCs, with ever increasing fund sizes, have been forced to become later stage (and life cycle) investors in companies that require large sums of capital in order to reach success. These are gross generalizations, but indicate what the trends are showing.

One result of this trend is what is often referred to as the 'funding gap' between angels and VCs. Traditionally, angels invest tens of thousands of dollars, or a few hundred thousand dollars in aggregate. With VCs now needing to invest a minimum of $10–20 million over the life of a portfolio company, there is a significant funding gap for companies looking for $500 000 to $2 million in capital. Angels and VCs are recognizing this gap as an opportunity. Angel groups are now syndicating deals between one another to raise ever larger rounds (in excess of $1–2 million), while VCs are using small 'feeder' funds to deploy $500 000 to $1 million for companies that either do not require large amounts of capital (for example, social media and Web 2.0 companies), or that enables them to have an option for putting in larger amounts of capital as the company progresses.

Why invest in early stage ventures? The greatest percentage increase in valuation in any company's life comes at the beginning – between the seed round and the first institutional round of financing. This is also the stage of greatest failure!

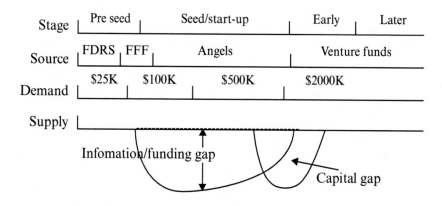

Source: Sohl, J. (2008), Center for Venture Research, University of New Hampshire (with permission).

Figure 3.3   The funding gap.

DYNAMICS OF AN ECOSYSTEM FOR TECHNOLOGICAL ENTREPRENEURSHIP

Many governments have attempted to create centers of excellence to promote innovation, company development and economic progress. Most of these attempts have failed because the geographical location of these centers did not have the key ingredients required to foster the commercialization of innovation. The Boston/Cambridge area has a dynamic ecosystem that fosters technological entrepreneurship. The key ingredients of this ecosystem include the following:

- Location – in the BankBoston study, location was a large determinant of technological innovation. Quality of life, access to skilled labor, proximity to markets, low business cost, access to universities, regulatory climate and tax rate were the top seven drivers of locating a business.
- Basic modern infrastructure – everything from wireless broadband Internet connection, to available real estate, to multiple transportation options constitute the basic requirements for modern commerce.
- Raw materials – in the case of Boston/Cambridge, smart and available human resources are just as critical as the universities from where they graduate. Students are the basic labor unit for a research

university, and can act as the greatest mechanism for technology transfer, which remains a 'full contact sport'.

- Fuel – sources of capital – angels and VCs – with open and active funds are the fuel to technology development. A cadre of service providers including lawyers, accountants, head hunters, consultants and real estate agents enable the development and function of all corporations.

- Spark – while the overall US economy is in flux, it is still a very large economy. Global markets are ever more accessible, and in certain times offer greater opportunity. Venture capital is a steady and growing asset class, so there is always a significant amount of capital flowing into early stage companies. Even in the face of lagging IPO activity, investors are seeing attractive exit opportunities for companies via merger and acquisition.

Do All the Players in the Value Chain Get Along?

The notion of 'good citizenship' is no more important than in the commercialization of university innovation. Sure, there is competition within each of the key connection points. VCs are always looking for the best deal before any other VC. Entrepreneurs vie for CEO positions. But, like every successful industry value chain, the individual players must cooperate and integrate. Below is a quick, and obvious, review of what motivates the various players in the Boston area innovation ecosystem.

Universities (professors, students, licensing offices)
Faculty at major research universities like MIT are motivated by scholarly pursuit, scientific discovery and using both of these capabilities to provide a dynamic learning environment for students – who are at university to learn. Having said that, many universities capitalize on scientific discovery through technology licensing. Faculties are stimulated to participate in that process by the economic benefits that ultimately accrue to the university through royalty payments – which, in MIT's case, are shared generously with inventors. Many faculties also generate additional income through consulting with industry, and by participating as founders of startup companies. While academic pursuits are primary, the economic benefits that result from commercialization of innovation is embraced.

Entrepreneurs
There is no doubt that entrepreneurs are motivated by economic gain – and the larger the opportunity the better. However, entrepreneurs have a

very special DNA. They typically have 'obsessive' personalities, prefer not to work for other people, thrive on the chaos of an early stage company and are driven by a passion to make it succeed. They need to convince employees to work for little pay, but with a big equity opportunity. They need to convince sources of capital – angels and VCs – that a significant return will be achieved. They need to develop a service or a product that has unique qualities for the market. They need to make customers believe this product or service to be a 'must have' rather than a 'nice to have'. This set of capabilities is rather daunting. After all, success or failure of the company is securely attached to their shoulders. This requires a unique individual.

Angels
Angels are a significant source of capital for early stage companies. Many angels are former entrepreneurs who have done well. Many are successful 'big' business people. Some have family wealth. All angels are looking for a significant financial return on their investment. However, most are interested in 'giving back' by mentoring entrepreneurs. Many are 'looking for something useful to do'. Angel groups are a relatively new phenomenon, starting in the mid-1990s to help individual angels leverage off the expertise and capital of others. There are now more than 250 angel groups in the USA, with 12 in the Boston area. While most still have a model where each individual makes their own decision, and writes their own check, some are organized as funds which act like mini-venture capital companies. These groups are also syndicating deals to one another on a regional basis to move upstream and provide larger amounts of capital to fill the funding gap. Angels appreciate the innovation from universities, but most do not fund 'students' who are starting companies, instead preferring seasoned management teams. Because many angels are successful entrepreneurs, they are excellent sources of CEOs. Angels and VCs have a love-hate relationship. VCs tend to discount the utility of angels who do not provide as much capital as they do, and typically do not follow their money like VCs. Angels can complicate a capitalization table, and terms are often a difficult discussion point as companies seek VC money after raising rounds with angels. On the other hand, angels tend to be more available, and have more operational experience. Nonetheless, VCs and angels are still reliant on each other.

Venture Capitalists
VCs are looking for huge capital gains for their funds. With very high fees to their investors (2 per cent management fee, 20 per cent incentive fee), they must produce attractive returns. With larger and larger fund sizes, VCs

are putting more and more capital to work. This has the benefit of allow-ing for life cycle investments, but has also prevented VCs from investing in companies with low capital requirements – like many of today's Web 2.0 companies. Because most VCs focus on very specific sectors, they have tremendous knowledge about companies in these sectors. That does not, however, imply that all VCs have a high level of operational expertise. The VC business has become more difficult as the US economy has fluctuated wildly in the last two decades. The IPO markets which are ever so impor-tant for VCs, have been poor in the last decade. Sure, there have been some huge, celebrated IPOs – think Google and eBay – but most exits are through merger and acquisition. More recently, slow markets have created greater difficulty as companies trim the products and service budgets, and have less ability to acquire companies at significant premiums. These are all gross generalizations, but are noted as trends.

Corporations

Corporations are searching for competitive advantage from any source – internal expertise, purchasing products and services for efficiency and growth, accessing external innovation through supporting research or corporate venturing and through acquisition of other companies. In this regard, companies are agnostic as to the source of innovation. They are the true buyer in the market, and as such play perhaps the most critical role in the innovation ecosystem. When economic times are poor – as they are currently in the USA – the returns to academ-ics, entrepreneurs, angels and VCs are dampened. Fortunately, many non-US economies are doing well. And given the global nature of commerce, there seems to be a market opportunity available some-where to support innovation.

Areas of Greatest Innovation

As noted above, venture capital investments in the USA in 2007 were nearly $30 billion, while angel investors made more than $26 billion in investments. So where is all this capital flowing to, and what are the next areas of opportunity? The University of New Hampshire's Center for Venture Research (UNH CVR) is an excellent resource for information about angel investing in the USA. According to the UNH CVR, software, healthcare services/medical devices and biotech have attracted more than 50 per cent of capital for each of the last three years. In 2007 software attracted 27 per cent, healthcare services/medical devices 19 per cent and biotech 12 per cent. The fastest growing sectors are energy and the Internet (Web 2.0, social websites and so on).

Angel investments were largely geared toward young companies, with nearly 40 per cent of all investments going to seed and startup companies. What is perhaps more interesting is the fact that more angels are also investing in expansion and later stage companies. There are two factors in play here that should be mentioned. First, some angel groups are organized as funds or special purpose vehicles that allow the use of follow-on capital reserves to support companies throughout their lifetime – not just in the startup phase. In addition, angel groups are acting more like VCs by syndicating opportunities to other groups. Boston makes for a very good example of this point, where the 20+ angel groups in New England (Maine, Vermont, New Hampshire, Massachusetts, Rhode Island and Connecticut) meet on a regular basis to present companies that they are already funding to raise additional, and larger capital, from their fellow angel groups.

In the short term it is likely that the sectors above continue to gain the lion's share of angel capital. Software has always been a big target. And while energy is one of the fastest growing sectors for venture capital, angels have a difficult time finding opportunities that have low capital requirements. Web 2.0 companies, however, are becoming quite popular in the angel space precisely because they have low capital requirements. The difficulty with investing in these companies is threefold. First, the revenue models are not well understood. Second, angels tend to be from an older demographic – they have little experience in Web-based companies and are not typically the target market either. Third, the barriers to entry for competitors are largely non-existent.

SUMMARY

Innovation – and the commercialization of that innovation – in the Cambridge/Boston area is akin to any mature industry where each piece of the value chain is occupied and optimized. Research universities in the area are an absolutely vital cog in generating new ideas. Schools like MIT have for 60 years worked closely with industry such that it is part of the DNA to consider the commercial applications of new technologies. Internal structures such as the more than 100 interdisciplinary research centers, Technology Licensing Office, Deshpande Center, Entrepreneurship Program, Industrial Liaison Program, Venture Mentoring Service, $100K Competition Prize and Enterprise Forum each play a vital role in stimulating students, faculty and researchers to commercialize the results of their research. Close ties with angels, VCs, entrepreneurs, companies and service providers further moves innovation to the commercial markets.

There is little friction in this innovation value chain. Each player has optimized their role, and receives just reward for their activities. There are few locations in the USA and beyond where such a dynamic ecosystem of innovation exists – and MIT is clearly at the epicenter of innovation in the Boston/Cambridge area.

NOTE

1. Enacted in 1980, the US Federal Bayh-Dole Act allows universities to retain title to inventions made under federally funded research programs.

BIBILIOGRAPHY

Ayers, Wayne M. (1997), *MIT: The Impact of Innovation*, Boston, MA: BankBoston.

Sohl, Jeffrey (2008), 'Center for venture research', presentation to University of New Hampshire.

Vest, C. et al. (2003), *Engines of Economic Growth: The Economic Impact of Boston's Eight Research Universities on the Metropolitan Boston Area*, New York: Appleseed.

Wright, Randall (2008), 'How to get the most from university relationships', *MIT Sloan Management Review*, **49** (3), 75–80.

4. The role of angel funds in early stage start-ups

Maurice Olivier

INVESTING IN EARLY STAGE VENTURES

Early stage ventures have a variety of crucial needs in marketing, technology, product development, leadership, human resources and, last but not least, financing. There are several types of investors who take an active interest in those ventures.

At one end of the spectrum, individual angel investors (or 'business angels') dominate seed investing and play an essential role in start-up investing. Available statistics show that they invest in total as much as, if not more than, institutional venture capital (VC) funds – and are involved in many more venture deals. They meet many of the needs of early stage companies as a result of their willingness to invest small amounts, their ability to decide and react quickly, and the knowledge and experience in industry or functional areas of relevance that they can bring to bear. But they quickly reach their own limits in terms of their propensity to invest, time available and deployable expertise. Typically, angel investors would invest no more than €0.5 million in any single round of capital. In spite of the rapid development of active business angel networks, which aim to channel the angel investment process in an organized and more cooperative way, their mode of working remains highly fragmented and individualistic – leading to frequent inactivity and high turnover. Finally, notwithstanding their willingness to help, they are seldom able to deploy the full range of skills that are required by rapidly growing start-ups.

At the other end of the spectrum, structured VC funds take an active part in financing 'second stage', more mature start-ups. However, many VC firms are not well-suited to participate in early stage investing, and may be reluctant to do so for several reasons that hinge on the economics of VC investment. The preparation and processing of transactions aimed at early stage companies and the post-investment monitoring of such companies demand significant amounts of time and efforts relative to the size of the deals, which inevitably eats into the compensation of the general partners of the funds. As the incentive grows to increase both the size of the funds and that of the deals to be pursued, the sheer amount of capital raised may become too big to justify devoting a sizable part of it to early stage investment. Lastly, over the past decade, the history of returns relative to risks for early stage investing has not been a very convincing one, except for the best-managed or luckiest funds. Consequently, many successful VCs are abandoning early stage investing, without being replaced by a surge of new funds aiming at the same investment stage. There is, therefore, a shortage of well-managed smaller funds to cover the 'equity gap' for investment rounds in the range of 0.7–2.5 million euros, which remains largely underoccupied.

By contrast, angel funds are well-suited to fill the €0.7–2.5 million investment gap. Angel funds typically gather between 20 and 40 individuals (often called 'members' below), who commit the same amount or amounts of similar magnitude, and join forces to invest in a structured manner following well-defined resource-sharing decision and organization processes. Although the legal form and the internal processes of the funds may vary considerably, their collective nature is distinctive both from that of individual investors and general partners-led VC organizations. Angel funds have been in existence and quite active in the USA and the UK for at least two decades; there are still very few of them in Continental Europe.

As a rule, well-managed angel funds can gradually build and deploy most of what VCs typically offer. First, contrary to early fears, in spite of the number of individuals involved, angel funds are typically quick to adopt a strict business orientation and focus on the economics of transactions. While they often originate from pre-existing looser 'ad hoc' investment structures, the angel funds can rapidly put in place stable, long-lasting legal and management structures, and collect funding in a reliable and reputable manner so as to reach a scale that enables them to become visible in the early stage capital market. After testing the waters in some early pilot deals, an angel fund would start attracting well-qualified requests for investment from entrepreneurs, banks, consultants, agents and so on. As soon as it can effectively demonstrate its own distinctive contribution to potential transactions by drawing on its members' experience, expertise and network, and prove it has enough financial strength to take part in later rounds of funding, the other VCs may come to consider it as a quasi-equal member of the VC community, and call upon it to take part in syndicate deals. Over time, the fund may even take a lead investor's role for certain projects. Of course, the ultimate acceptance test lies in the angel fund's ability to groom investee companies and successfully execute profitable exits.

But angel funds distinguish themselves by the specific characteristics and benefits they can bring to bear. First, angel funds are by construct low-cost organizations that draw on the combined resources of their members and involve them collectively in various actions. In doing so, they are bound to at least partially overcome the cost disadvantage associated with the smaller size of the investment deals and overall funding resources. Members typically include successful cashed-out entrepreneurs, seasoned managers, high-level bankers, lawyers, professionals and so on who have the skills – individually and collectively – and hopefully the time to thoroughly investigate and appraise potential investment deals in the course of the due diligence process. The funds are able to reach investment decisions without undue delay, as would their members if they were to invest on their own. In addition, the funds provide a unique pool of talent, expertise and experience from which to draw for the post-investment coaching and guidance of the portfolio companies, including when a replacement or complementary management for the investee company must be found. The funds are thus able to provide 'lead angel investors' to the investees as board members, mentors or business developers. Finally, angel groups can demonstrate the value added brought to the regional or national economy and easily attract the sympathy of government institutions, which see them as fulfilling a useful economic role and covering needs that are insufficiently met otherwise.

Although available data is sketchy to date, well-managed angel funds, that is, those that invest well and prudently and keep costs under control, are likely to achieve VC-like internal rates of return as shown from particular cases in the USA or the UK.

However, in order to deliver their full potential, angel funds need the right structure, management, decision processes, investment rules and compensation schemes, and a creative way to harness the wealth of the collective talents that are present in their members' 'pool'. How this can be accomplished is the subject of the next section, after which a case example is presented.

STRUCTURING AN ANGEL FUND

Member-led vs Manager-led Organizations

Angel funds can be structured as member-led or manager-led organizations although a broad continuum exists between the two forms.

In a member-led organization members would share the work of deal sourcing, carrying out the due diligences, negotiating, closing the deals, investee monitoring and, in parallel, membership recruitment and management, and members' training. Neither important upfront investment nor sizable recurrent expenditures are needed – modest membership dues, fees charged to candidates or investee companies and contributions by selected sponsors can cover most of the administrative costs and support.

The main challenges of a member-led organization are manifold. Those members who volunteer or are the most capable may become indispensable and be called in over and over to make things work, thus running a high risk of 'burn-out'. A range of committees must be set up to deal with the various aspects of managing the fund, but they may soon face sparse attendance and may become ineffective, leading to inconsistent decisions and patchy investee monitoring. After some time, the interests and priorities of the leaders may deviate from those of the other investors. Hence it should be no surprise that only those organizations that are strongly bound together under the leadership of dedicated and highly respected leaders-investors survive in the longer term.

In a manager-led organization one or several professional manager(s) (also called 'general partners') coordinate with the members the various tasks of sourcing, diligence, deal structuring, portfolio monitoring, membership issues and so on. Most typically, those managers take direct responsibility for the tasks that cannot be executed in a large group or require advanced skills or knowledge, such as valuing and closing the deals, providing guidance to the members or managing the exits. The benefits of bringing in and empowering professional 'outsiders' are obvious. Operations are managed professionally, with a clear focus on investment economics. The time and collective energy of the members are channeled towards the most important and urgent tasks, and appropriate oversight is given to crucial processes, such as the analysis of new prospects or the due diligence effort.

This type of organization is not without its own challenges. First, significant financial resources must be set apart to compensate the managers both with a recurring compensation and long-term incentives. Because of the relatively small size of the funds, the compensation may, however, turn out to be too thin to attract and keep the best managers, even on a part-time basis. Also, the services and attention demanded by the members and the task of managing the membership may be exceedingly time-consuming, with the risk that the managers will drift their focus away from priority investment tasks. Clearly, only funds beyond a minimum size and with sufficiently tight discipline are bound to be profitable for their members and managers.

Investment Process and Decision-making

Should the fund's key investment decisions be made by the managers, ad hoc committees or a collegial decision-making process involving all the members? Experience shows that when most decisions are made by the managers or by an ad hoc 'investment committee' – a solution akin to that adopted by most VCs – there is high risk that the individual members become disfranchised, even if the committee members are regularly rotated. This leads to suboptimal use and leverage of the talent pool comprised of the members-investors, who typically have accumulated a wealth of experience and skills over their professional life as successful entrepreneurs and managers, and are ready to put them to use for the benefit of the fund.

It is hence widely believed that angel funds work best if the members themselves make many of the essential decisions through a majority voting process that takes place in actual meetings. Such key decisions include whether or not to engage in a due diligence effort with respect to a candidate investee company, and – more importantly – whether to actually proceed with an investment in a given project based on the conclusions of the due diligence team.

The members' active participation in the key decision schemes enhances their involvement in the life of the fund in a variety of manners. First, it stimulates them to be physically present at the meetings in which entrepreneurs are invited to introduce their new prospective projects, and to make educated decisions, at times after lively debates, about which projects are worth following up and which must be rejected. Second, it motivates them to take an active part, in turn and on a voluntary basis, in the due diligence teams in light of the specific skills (functional, industrial, managerial, cross-national and so on) each of them can bring to bear. The active involvement of the members in the due diligence process is, without any question, the keystone of a well-functioning angel fund – it helps to keep the overall cost level of the fund down, and can significantly contribute to the quality of the investment analysis and review. Finally, the direct participation of the members, under the guidance and leadership of the fund managers, in the decision to proceed or not with an investment after openly debating the pros and cons based on the conclusions of the due diligence team, substantially enriches the decision process and improves its quality, depth, reliability and perhaps overall wisdom. Usually, however, the proposed detailed terms of the deal are shared with the members but not submitted to vote, so as to leave sufficient freedom to the fund managers to negotiate the final terms and conditions.

As can be expected, managing the active involvement of a group of, say, 30 individual members-investors requires clear rules, well-mastered group dynamics, a close interaction with the members both in the formal meetings and informal exchanges, and a fair amount of leadership-cum-diplomacy. Also, it is important that most, if not all, participants reach a minimum level of proficiency and 'professionalism' in the key disciplines of VC investment. This can be achieved through formal training sessions, and even more effectively by learning in the field from their peers and the fund's managers in the course, for example, of the due diligence process.

Equal vs Free Investment Amounts

One of the early decisions to be made in drawing the charter of an angel fund is whether the members-investors are required to invest the same amount in the fund or not. An 'egalitarian' investment scheme fosters the personal commitment and cohesiveness of the members, and motivates them to remain personally involved in the most important decisions to be made throughout the life of the fund.

As an alternative, the investment amounts may be allowed to vary across members. This, however, may become the source of tensions and frustrations between them and complicate the task of the managers if the larger investors demand a bigger say in the functioning of the fund.

Between these two extremes, a range of practical schemes can be implemented aimed at combining the '*esprit de corps*' that goes along with an equal participation with the need to providing the members with an opportunity to invest greater amounts in those projects that attract them most. One of the most effective solutions to add a dose of investment flexibility is to authorize the members, usually against a separate arrangement fee, to directly co-invest in the investee projects. Later on, this may spark tension between the 'most successful' and the 'least successful' investors, since we all know that only a few 'home-runs' will eventually be achieved, and a number of co-investors may thus end up in a single-digit internal rate of return or be money losers. In any case, it is recommended that all co-investors in any given project should invest through a single legal structure so as to avoid multiplying the number of shareholders. Which legal and fiscal structure is best suited for this purpose is heavily country-dependent.

One of the key problems, however, is that angel funds that would rely solely on the financial contribution of individual investors would in most cases remain below critical size. Imagine a contribution of 100 000 euros each by 30 individuals, and a co-investment in the range of 1:1 (that is, for each euro invested by the angel fund, the members would invest another euro directly or through a distinct common structure). The total 'operational' scale of the fund is €6.0 million, which, honorable as it might be particularly for a first fund, is hardly enough to reward the managers of the fund, access the better deals and build a recognizable brand. Raising the number of investors or the minimal investment threshold is feasible, but only within limits. In view of this, angel funds may decide to look for a limited number of additional non-angel investors, such as small family offices or funds, banks, regional investment funds and so on. These investors may be attracted by the 'transparent' structure and functioning of the angel fund, the relatively small amounts to be committed (say, between 5 and 20 times those committed by the individual investors) and the opportunity to co-invest directly in the investee companies. The key challenge then lies in the capacity of the fund to absorb those 'larger-scale' investors while keeping up the spirit and the mechanisms of an 'angel' organization. A possible solution is to bring the non-angel investors to agree to having just the same voting power as any individual angel member, save some truly fundamental decisions (such as the general strategy of the fund, the replacement of a general manager and so on.).

Compensating the Managers

In the case of manager-led funds, one of the most crucial issues is the fund's ability to attractively compensate the managers. With this in view, the fund must both collect short-term revenues distributable to the managers and provide them with a long-term contingent incentive in the form of a carried interest scheme. Short-term revenues may come from a range of sources. The two most common sources are an annual management fee on capital committed (for example, 1–3 per cent per annum in the first years and then decreasing after the closing of the investment period), which is a typical VC scheme, and arrangement fees, that is, a percentage of the investment amount to be paid by the investee (if this is legal in the country concerned) or by the investors (for example, 2–5 per cent). The angel fund may also charge investee candidates for filing and presenting their project to the fund, charge a fee to cover the due diligence and legal costs or have them reimbursed by the investee, invoice post-investment monitoring fees to the portfolio companies (for example, 1–2 per cent per annum), receive board membership fees (usually to be shared with the individual members acting as board members), seek affiliation or sponsoring fees from 'friendly' institutions (such as banks, consultants, industry associations or even non-competing VC organizations) and so on. Of course, not all the above schemes are mutually compatible, and some may have a negative effect. For example, funds that seek excessive amounts from outside sponsors may damage their reputation and be suspected of relinquishing their independence, and those that are known to charge disproportionate amounts to investee companies may lose access to the best deals.

Longer term, the managers are to be offered a carried interest in the range of 10 to 20 per cent of the capital gains realized by the fund upon the occurrence of exits, a scheme typical of the VC industry, which ensures the alignment of their long-term financial interests with those of the investors.

Relationship with Angel Networks

The relationship between the angel fund and the associated angel network(s), where they exist, is another issue to be addressed at the outset. The interactions and overlaps are multiple. Many angel funds emanate from existing angel 'matching' networks and share with them some of their managers, staff or premises. Also, many of the angel fund investors may have been active members of the 'source' angel network before joining the fund, and may want to remain members of this network so as to continue to explore other projects individually. Furthermore, while the angel funds would typically be targeting 'first stage' investment deals and commit higher amounts than any ad hoc group of individual angels, the divide may not always be as clear-cut. Many projects, when first identified, may be seen as candidates both for angel investing and angel fund investing.

To avoid damaging conflicts, it is recommended to agree which organization will take the lead in view of the situation. If a project is first presented to the network but is then seen as exceeding the means of individual investors, it should be referred to the angel fund's management, and vice versa if the project is not sufficiently mature to meet the angel fund's criteria. Experience shows that a smooth relationship and transparent exchange rules between the two organizations are beneficial to both. Also, it is not infrequent that the angel fund would call upon the angel network to help to close a deal that is still insufficiently funded after the angel fund co-investors have indicated how much they are committed to investing.

At any rate, the two organizations must be kept distinct. Angel fund investors invest both their time and money in making the angel fund work, and they expect to receive a great deal in return, including high-quality sourcing, professional due diligence reports and well-formed investment decisions leading to successful exits. In contrast, individual business angels are not requested to invest any resources in their network organization, and essentially expect to be introduced to potentially good projects, which they then will review in small groups or on their own, and invest in against one-time arrangement fees charged by the network. Those are two very distinct models, and in the absence of clear rules and limits there might be too great an incentive for individual business angels to 'piggy-back' on the angel fund's projects without having to support the true cost of the investment process.

Legal/Fiscal Structure

Little of anything definite can be said about which legal or fiscal structure to adopt. The angel fund's structure should, of course, reflect the philosophy and the agreement between the members, and be as tax efficient as local laws permit for the investors. The legal documents must be drawn up carefully so as to avoid that the active involvement of the members in the functioning of the fund gives rise to a legal or fiduciary responsibility exceeding that of limited partners. Another element to be considered is whether the angel fund may remain eligible for the various support schemes (grants, tax deductions, investment insurance, co-investment facilities and so on) that are increasingly made available to early stage individual angel investors. The problem of selecting the most suitable structure is also compounded by the fact that a tax efficient carried interest structure must be set up for the managers, or that the fund has various sources of income other than capital gains and interests from the investee companies. All in all, the solutions will vary widely by country.

CASE STUDY: BAMS ANGELS FUND

BAMS Angels Fund was created in late 2005 and is based in Louvain-la-Neuve, Belgium. It brings together 30 'active' angels who each committed €100000 at the outset, and an additional €25000 in 2007, that is, a total of €125000 euros each. Each investor has one vote in the Investment Committee. About six months after the first closing, as the Fund was able to diffuse the skepticism of the VC community *vis-à-vis* what initially appeared as an unreliable organization managed by a mass of individuals, several institutional investors joined the Fund and increased its capital to about €7 million: a major international bank, a regional development agency and a Belgian-based family holding structure. Some 'matching' funds were also made available, for more than €1 million, from a federal agency. In spite of their higher contribution, the institutional investors were granted one representative each at the Investment Committee, and hence only one vote, except for very specific legal matters.

The Fund focuses on first stage investment and disregards seed and start-up projects. It typically invests around €500000 per project in the first round, with the individual members co-investing together an additional €300000–700000 in the same round against an arrangement fee of 2 to 4 per cent of the amount invested. Most frequently, the highest contributors among the co-investors are those that have actively taken part in the due diligence effort. On average, the co-investors double the investment made by the Fund, thus significantly increasing its visibility and bargaining power. The Fund intends to invest in about ten projects, a goal that should be achieved by the end of 2008, after which a Fund II will be launched.

The management team comprises three general partners dedicating about 40 per cent of their time to the Fund, who have access to secretarial support and external accounting resources. The management fee paid is 2.75 per cent per annum on capital committed for the first three years, which is then decreased to 1 per cent per annum of capital invested as of the fourth year, and the general partners are entitled to a carried interest of 20 per cent of the capital gains.

The Fund maintains a smooth and constant relationship with its 'sister' seed and start-up-oriented angel network organization, with which it shares one general partner. A limited number of the Fund's projects have been sourced from the angel network when they appeared to exceed the size or complexity that the network members could manage. Vice versa, several projects that turned out to be at a too early stage for the Fund at the close of the due diligence effort were referred back to the network and were funded by a mix of network members and individual Fund members investing on their own. Occasionally, the Fund has called for network members to complement a round of investment, usually for small amounts.

The Investment Committee is comprised of all the individual investors and one representative of each of the institutional investors. It meets about every six to seven weeks for three to four hours, with an average attendance rate in excess of 65 per cent. In each meeting two or three presentations of new candidate projects are made by entrepreneurs, after which the committee votes on whether to recommend engaging in a due diligence effort or not. After the due diligence is completed, the results and recommendations are presented to the committee by the due diligence team members, and it is then the committee's responsibility to vote on whether to recommend an investment or reject it. While formally they are not binding, the management team has committed to strictly abiding by the Investment Committee's resolutions.

Typically, four to six due diligences are in progress at any time. Each due diligence team is led by one of the general partners and count between two and five of the Fund's members who take their fair share of the work in line with their skills, experience, knowledge and interests. While there is no strict rule, all members have participated in at least one due diligence since the inception of the Fund. Fully documented due diligence reports are sent to all members prior to the meeting of the Investment Committee.

Those members whose experience and interests are closest to a given field of activity – and who typically have taken part in the prior due diligence effort – then monitor the investee companies jointly with one of the general partners either as a board member or an observer to the board.

In summary, members take an active role in referring leads, conducting due diligences, debating the appropriateness and economics of each deal, voting investment decisions, and ensuring post-investment mentoring through board presence and specific tasks or missions. An Ethics Committee, independent from the management team, has been set up to issue guidelines on membership, conflicts of interest, interpretation of rules, valuation in case of forced departures and so on. The management team and also each of the Fund's members make it a priority to maintain good collective spirit and teamwork among all investors.

After about two and a half years of existence, the Fund has gained increasingly well-qualified deal referrals and built brand awareness with entrepreneurs, banks, VCs and government. The Fund has invested in syndication with several other VCs, both private and publicly funded, and acted on a few occasions as the lead investor.

MANAGING THE ANGEL FUND

As shown by the BAMS Angels Fund and other similar cases, the successful development of an angel fund requires a number of essential skills pertaining to the management of the internal organization, the external relations, the team of managers and, of course, the relationship with the investee companies. Those managerial aspects are addressed in this last section.

Probably the most important organizational challenge a management team (or the fund's chosen leaders, in the absence of a management team) faces is to ensure a business-like attitude and behavior among all members throughout the investment process while securing the tight and amicable relationships that make up the core flavor, conviviality and fun of the angel fund. Leadership and interpersonal skills are required to achieve a healthy cross-fertilization between the members, and an equal commitment to due diligence work through a 'fair' rotation of the participants. The managers must also provide formal education, role models and templates as needed. The full-group decision meetings should be prepared with care so as to reach decisions that are economically sensible and also satisfying for the members. As already mentioned, a key risk is that the management team may have at times to devote excessive efforts to coping with members-related tasks at the detriment of more essential analyses or decisions. The use of a dedicated exchange platform (such as Angelsoft or any equivalent system) to structure and disseminate the relevant information to the members at all stages of the investment process can prove quite helpful in this respect.

The managers are also the primary 'face' of the angel fund *vis-à-vis* the external world. In this regard, the managers' tasks are not different than those of any VC general partner, which is to maintain the volume and quality of deal sourcing and negotiate the best investment decisions with the right partners. The main difference is the need for the angel fund managers to promote the 'unique selling proposition' and distinctive advantages of the fund to initially skeptical entrepreneurs or syndicate investors who may be wary of the decision-making and sustainability of such a 'collegial' organization. This includes acquainting the candidate entrepreneurs and partnering investors with the decision-making process of the fund, which is by nature different than that followed by traditional VC organizations.

As is clear from the above, the task of the general partners of an angel fund is undoubtedly a demanding one. Of course, any VC management work is demanding, involving many years of strenuous effort from the launch of a fund to the last investee exit, with the reward becoming visible in the form of significant cash compensation only in the later years of the fund. However, the angel fund general partners are confronted in addition with the task of managing and guiding a large group of seasoned, sometimes hard-to-harness individuals. It should hence not be a surprise if some of the managers become tired and quit, particularly if their expected post-exit compensation does not appear adequate. Keeping the managers happy and focused on the task should remain a key concern for the formal or informal leaders of the investors' group.

Last but not least, the general partners of the fund have a key mandate to monitor the investee companies and make them fit for exit, which is never an easy task. In the 'equity gap' range, however, angel funds may have a clear advantage over many VCs through the sheer size and diversity of the internal talent pool they can tap to resolve many of the problems encountered at the investee level, thus providing benefits that VCs cannot. By combining a strict monitoring process closely led by the fund managers with the insight and experience of the members-investors, the angel funds may be in a favorable position to steer successful exits.

A PROGNOSIS

It is safe to predict that structured angel organizations such as angel funds will take on an increasing share of the €0.7–2.5 million equity investment range. As we have noted previously, while the concept has been applied successfully in the USA and the UK, there are still very few examples of note in Continental Europe. This is probably due to the tight economics of the business model, and to the reluctance, skepticism or the many failed attempts to get a large number of hard-nosed, experienced individuals to work closely and harmoniously together with the purpose of making sound investment decisions. It is to be foreseen that gradually best practices will emerge and more 'standardized' models will develop for angel funds, with a good dose of country specificity. When the first funds will start to exit, second and third generations of funds will be launched, many with the same managers and possibly the same investors. This will without any doubt contribute to enhancing the overall level of professionalism, consistency and repeatability within the angel fund community.

Being positioned between the individual business angels and the institutional VCs, angel funds are due to become a distinct segment of the private equity sector in their own right. This will hopefully occur without our having to relinquish the passion and the fun that are so characteristic of today's pioneering funds.

ACKNOWLEDGMENTS

This work draws on a presentation made by the author at the Advanced International Summer School 2007 seminar on 'Perspectives on technological entrepreneurship' organized by ISUFI, Università del Salento (Lecce, Italy) held in Ostuni, Italy in July 2007. The author thanks his colleagues and partners at BAMS Angels Fund, Louvain-la-Neuve, Belgium, who have provided invaluable insights into the build-up and functioning of an angel fund over several years. Early contributions by David Verrill, Founder and Managing Director of Hub Angel Investment Group, LLC in Newton, Massachusetts, were instrumental.

BIBLIOGRAPHY

Angel Capital Association, www.angelcapitalassociation.org.
Community Development Venture Capital Alliance, www.cdvca.org.
European Business Angel Network, www.eban.org.
Kauffman Foundation, www.emkf.org.
National Association of Seed and Venture Funds, www.nasvf.org.
National Venture Capital Association, www.nvca.org.
Note: All websites accessed 10 November, 2008.

5. The locus of innovation in small and medium-sized firms: the importance of social capital and networking in innovative entrepreneurship

Willem Hulsink, Tom Elfring and Wouter Stam

INTRODUCTION

The economist Giovanni Dosi (1988, p. 1132) made the point that innovation is primarily a process built on the activation of the specific internal capabilities, cumulative routines and implicit or tacit knowledge of established corporations: 'one needs to have substantial in-house capacity in order to recognise, evaluate, negotiate, and finally adapt the technology potentially available from others.' The driving forces behind innovation in these larger firms are internal employees and inputs from R&D, manufacturing or sales units and so on. Others have stressed the mobilization of external resources from the companies' environment, such as direct or indirect links with leading knowledge institutions, dedicated suppliers, customers and so on. Oerlemans et al. (1998) have argued that, in order to explain innovative performance, both internal and external resources need to be included. Entrepreneurial firms suffering from strong internal resource constraints or competency gaps may benefit from external linkages with technology partners, investors and/or service providers, acting as real complementors. Similarly, Lee et al. (2001) argued that networking with external parties providing complementary resources contributes to a further accumulation of internal capabilities. In this chapter we follow their advice and attempt to answer the following question: Which ties and network positions matter when it comes to complementing internal competences in order to be innovative? In other words, we investigate the role networks play in finding external knowledge that can be combined with internal competences to realize new combinations.

Our study involves an analysis of whether social and economic networks influence innovation processes or, as Oerlemans et al. (1998) put it: 'Do networks matter for innovation?', with an exclusive focus on the creation and implementation of new ideas, processes and products within and by small and medium-sized firms. The starting point in our study is the assumption that social networks play an important role in the innovation process. To promote new products, and to develop new markets and new ways of producing and distributing, the founders of new firms as well as corporate entrepreneurs who engage in strategic initiatives in established companies can draw upon extensive and rich personal and business contacts (Floyd and Woolridge, 1999; Stam and Elfring, 2008). These benefits stem from privileged access to knowledge, financial capital, legitimacy and other resources that facilitate entrepreneurial behaviour and performance. The efficient or effective use of social networks has been recognized as a key driver in the promotion and implementation of innovation. After all, 'innovation does not exist in a vacuum' (Van De Ven, 1986, p. 601). Especially in new and small and medium-sized enterprises (SMEs), innovation processes usually transcend the boundaries of a firm. External parties may be sources of inspiration and/or they may contribute to the implementation of innovations. Many SMEs have insufficient organizational resources, knowledge or capabilities to develop innovations by themselves. These are all reasons why smaller firms may seek larger parties for the purposes of collaboration.

On the one hand, the contacts a firm has can generate advantages for further innovation and growth while, on the other hand, they may lead to inertia and stagnation, for example, by being locked out from where the action is, taking the wrong advice or choosing the wrong partner or being locked into a leading firm, sector or cluster in decline. In the former case the existing social network or new business contact provides opportunities that may eventually lead to success, whereas in the latter case the existing network or new business contacts turn out to have a constraining or even detrimental effect on a firm's performance. The search and use of social capital is driven by goal specificity: it only includes those ties that help the actor attain particular goals. To date, most studies have been deliberately or accidentally one-sided, for example, by focusing exclusively on entrepreneurial firms in dynamic industries (or more specifically on start-ups in the high-tech industries), or by paying selective attention either to the internal sources or to the external contacts to trigger innovation. In cases where the impact of internal and external ties on innovation have both been examined the sample often includes large and established companies and managers (rather than entrepreneurs and smaller firms, on which our study focuses).

Before taking a more detailed look at relevant existing studies, we formulate a number of basic assumptions that indicate our starting point and research approach. Firstly, networks do not make or break ideas, products, people or firms, nor do they have any discretionary power. By opening up opportunities or pre-selecting a life course of firms and by imposing constraints on their discretion, networks provide a context for social action. Secondly, the level of analysis in this study is the entrepreneur and/or his firm, and their personal and business-related networks. Although in the ideation and formation phase the entrepreneur and his company are a single entity, when a company starts to grow and hires new people, they start to diverge. In that case, the social network of the entrepreneur and that of his firm may be different. In addition, employees infuse the company with additional social capital and may bring useful contacts, such as leads to new suppliers, customers and knowledge institutions.

Thirdly, there is the temporal dimension of social networks. Exchanging information, building trust and pooling resources are not things that develop overnight, but networking is an ongoing process. Social networks gradually unfold (and sometimes diminish) over a long period of time, only occasionally interrupted by events or incidents, such as opportunities for or threats to the firm, that require decisive and immediate social action. Too often, in network analysis a static view of social capital and network development is adopted, while the time span used is too short. This may result in a bias in which infrequent relations may be overlooked and latent or dormant ties may be mistakenly treated as still active. Networking is a dynamic process, in which latent ties may become manifest, and manifest ties may become dormant, depending on the situation in which the firm finds itself and the urgency of action (Hite, 2003). Old bonds, new ties or dormant contacts may be activated, surpassing the existing network to meet the need and support the survival and growth of the company.

Another observation is that social networking is not necessarily a good and positive thing. Many researchers argue that social networks, a term that is often used interchangeably with related terms like (inter-organizational) trust and reciprocity, are to be preferred to the chaotic and fluid market place and rigid bureaucracies. Falling back on one's friends and relatives, finding new leads and resources through former colleagues, using external consultants, participating in trade fairs, contacting other local entrepreneurs and attending seminars are all useful in the search for information and mobilization of resources. However, it is not the quantity of the ties and the amount of networking *per se* that is relevant. Rather, it is the quality, objective and timing of the social networking that are crucial in the evolution of a firm or entrepreneur. In addition to the potential danger of network overload, network closure and lock-in can also be seen as less positive sides of networks. Uzzi (1997) has, for example, referred to the dangers of the 'overembeddedness' of relationships, in which firms are insulated from new knowledge and find it harder to adapt to new circumstances.

The main line of reasoning in this chapter is as follows. In the following section we discuss the key network concepts, including social capital, relational embeddedness (strong and weak ties) and structural embeddedness (the so-called 'structural holes' in the large social community). Next, we address innovation and the central role of knowledge in the discovery and realization of innovations. Because networks and their potential for knowledge brokering appear to be important, we close by focusing on the relationship between particular network characteristics and innovation.

NETWORKING: LOOKING FOR AND USING SOCIAL CAPITAL

Gabbay and Leenders (1999, p. 3) define 'corporate social capital' as 'the set of resources, tangible or virtual, that accrue to a corporate player through the player's social relationships, facilitating the attainment of goals'. The assets from which entrepreneurs or entrepreneurial teams in deal making and competition are embedded within and made available through social networks, or alternatively the assets entrepreneurs look for to strengthen their strategic position, may be found in new social networks and through 'networking'. As a consequence of new legislation or shifts in technology and demand, entrepreneurs may realize that there is a gap between the currently available social capital and the social capital required to cope with new demands or opportunities. The response could include a combination of human capital (for example, more and better education and training of present staff and hiring new employees), financial capital (for example, negotiating a bank loan or a deal with a venture capitalist) and social capital (for example, recruiting a new senior manager, approaching new customers and so on).

Like other forms of capital, social capital is a productive force that makes it possible, for example, to achieve goals that would otherwise not be attainable. Human, physical and financial capital refers to the possession of knowledge, equipment and money on the part of an actor or group of actors. Social capital does not reside in a person's skills and diplomas, power over tools and materials, or control over funds, but it is embedded in social ties and networks. Some people argue that social capital can be located in a person's address book, hence the term 'Rolodex power'. Human, physical and financial capital are different from social capital in at least two ways: in terms of ownership and in terms of contribution to productivity (Burt, 1992). While the former three forms of capital are owned (and to some extent controlled) by individuals, groups or organizations, social capital is owned by the players making up the relationship, with none of them in possession of the exclusive property rights. While the investment of human, physical and human capital will have a direct effect on the production capabilities, the availability of social capital is a necessary but not sufficient enabler of growth and innovation. The deployment of social capital will have only an indirect effect on performance, running through the contacts and networks generating the opportunities and the necessary resources. The search for and use of social capital is sometimes the outcome of a deliberate encounter between an actor and new contacts (for example, at trade fairs and conferences), but it is often the by-product of other activities (for example, shared background at high school, work, sport clubs). In fact, actors may not even be aware of the value of their social capital: the social structure in which they are embedded may contain information, resources and advantages of which they are unaware (for example, the children of successful entrepreneurs).

In their work on 'corporate social capital and liability', Leenders and Gabbay (1999) pay attention to the positive and negative effects of social networks in relation to the realization of goals of small and medium-sized firms and their leaders. Most studies on social networks are extremely positive, arguing that 'networks are good, more networks are better' and supportive social ties help people get jobs, pay rises and faster promotion. Leenders and Gabbay's book is one is of the few works that offers a balanced approach to the ambiguous effects of social ties and structures: on the one hand, they facilitate the search for information, opportunities and resources (that is, positive social capital) while, on the other hand, constraining or even impeding the attainment of goals (social liability, also called negative social capital). In this respect, Gargiulo and Benassi (1999) (included in the Leenders and Gabbay volume) refer to the bright and dark side of social capital: in the case of a start-up firm, strong ties provided by close relatives, friends and former colleagues could be beneficial at the inception stage (for example, in terms of providing emotional support, money, business recipes), but they could become a liability with regard to future expansion. The company may lack the selfishness, innovativeness and opportunity-seeking focus that is needed at a later stage. For example, in the case of ethnic entrepreneurship dense networks can have supporting and yet oppressive effects: ethnic entrepreneurs who are already short on the vital business contacts outside their local cultural community (for example, useful weak ties with banks, chambers of commerce) may suffocate even more by the particularistic demands posed by the strong ties that have initially provided them with access to essential resources.

The structure of networks may vary from a loose collection of ties to close-knit business groups in which the focal organization is strongly embedded. Granovetter (1973) has specified the intensity and diversity of relationships, that is, the difference between strong and weak ties, on the basis of four criteria: the frequency of contacts, the emotional intensity of the relationship, the degree of intimacy and reciprocal commitments between the actors involved. While weak ties provide access to (new) industry information and to new business contacts, strong tries are relationships that can be relied on at all times. Strong ties tend to bind similar people in longer term and intense relationships. Affective ties with close friends and relatives may provide a short cut to or even preclude the search for useful knowledge and access to critical resources. In other words, strong ties contribute to 'economies of time' (Uzzi, 1997, p. 49): the ability to capitalize quickly on market opportunities. The manifestation of strong ties will also reduce the time spent on monitoring and bargaining over agreements: free-riding behaviour will be discouraged and transaction costs reduced. Strong ties are more likely to be useful in situations characterized by high levels of uncertainty and insecurity, for example, with radical innovations. In such complex settings individuals rely on close friends and relatives for protection, uncertainty reduction and mutual learning. Krackhardt (1992) has elaborated on the affective component of strong ties by arguing that commitment, loyalty and friendship within an organization will be critical to that organization's ability to deal with major crises. In short, a social structure based on strong ties will promote the development of trust, the transfer of fine-grained information and tacit knowledge, and joint problem-solving (Uzzi, 1997; Rowley et al., 2000).

In situations of high uncertainty researchers found not only benefits of strong ties, but also limitations. The limitations have to do with the ability to discover information on opportunities to improve the business model of the start-up. In the initial stages start-ups continuously search for improvements in the way they combine resources in order to satisfy demand in a profitable way. In those situations weak ties appear to be more beneficial than strong ties when it comes to searching for new information. Burt (1992) elaborates on the strength of weak ties hypothesis (Granovetter, 1973) and argues paradoxically that the absence of ties, or more precisely, selective network autonomy (that is, actors who are connected to disconnected others) may even provide an advantage. In Burt's social network theory a large diverse network is the best guarantee of having a contact present where useful information is aired. The availability of so-called structural holes in a social network generates an even better pay-off: a structural hole is a relationship of non-redundancy between two contacts (redundant: leading to the same people and thus providing the same information benefits) (Burt, 1992). Burt's advice to improve one's capital is crystal clear: players should invest in non-redundant ties and disinvest redundant relationships.

The weak versus strong tie discussion refers to relational embeddedness. In the existing literature a distinction is drawn between relational and structural embeddedness. Relational embeddedness refers to the characteristics of the relationships, such as strength and content: for example, strong or weak ties. Structural embeddedness has to do with the structure of a network, or in particular the position of the firm (or person) within the network structure. The characteristics of the network structure have been described as being either dense or sparse, while the 'structural' position of a firm or person within a network has been described by referring to, for example, centrality or a position rich in structural holes (that is, allowing for arbitrage and strategic advantage seeking). Although both relational and structural embeddedness may affect firm performance, within both dimensions research has thus far remained inconclusive. In the next section we look at the various studies and their findings concerning the beneficial effects of particular network characteristics. In any case, empirical evidence suggests that strong ties are beneficial to a firm's performance (including the degree of innovativeness), while in some cases weak ties also appear to be very important. Similarly, some researchers argue in favour of dense networks, while others favour sparse networks. In addition, centrality has great intuitive appeal as being favourable to innovation; in the last decade, however, the concept of structural holes has drawn most attention in relation to the discovery of new information and knowledge. Since new information and the ability to find new knowledge appear to be crucial to innovation, the structural hole argument has great potential, which is why we discuss it in greater detail.

The structural hole argument has to do with information advantages that benefit people who build across cohesive groups, exploiting a position on the intersection between two groups. In addition to benefiting from brokering the flow of information between people, structural holes also allow entrepreneurs to benefit from the subtle control of projects that bring together people who are not (yet) connected. In the structural holes theory three concepts play a central role: brokerage, entrepreneurship and structural holes. Brokerage includes an early and efficient access to valuable information and referrals to new contacts. According to Burt (1992, p. 354), an entrepreneur is 'a person who generates profit from being between others'. Eventually, being close to the social holes and benefiting from them through arbitrage pays off (Burt, 1992): it implies being exposed to diverse sources of information and subsequently having a better chance to gain access to good ideas. Also, firms with a more heterogeneous mix of alliance partners enjoy faster revenue growth and tend to obtain more obtaining patents; similarly, managers with a network that has been optimized for structural holes are rewarded with better compensation, performance evaluations and faster promotions.

INNOVATION AND KNOWLEDGE BROKERING

Innovation can be described as the discovery of new ideas and concepts, new combinations and new organizational approaches, often resulting in new products or processes and sometimes to the formation of new ventures. Innovation is often portrayed as an iterative, cumulative and interactive process, involving all kinds of learning: learning by doing, learning by using and learning by interacting (Quinn et al., 1997; March, 1991). Elaborating on Schumpeter's notions of creative destruction and new combinations, Weick (1979, pp. 252–3) has defined creativity as 'putting old things into new combinations and new things into old combinations. In either case, novel relations between pairs of things are the essence of creativity.' The process of innovation typically transcends the boundaries of existing firms, industries and populations of organizations.

Knowledge brokering and learning for innovation can be studied at various levels of analysis. Firstly, we take a look at the network level. A key conceptual contribution to this level of analysis is the 'locus of innovation' study by Powell et al. (1996). Hargadon and Sutton (1997) examine a similar issue from the point of view of the individual firm and investigate how knowledge brokering through network ties contributes to the realization of innovations. We first discuss the contribution by Powell and associates, followed by a summary of the findings of the various studies by Hargadon.

In their research into the locus of innovation Powell et al. (1996) have applied a social network approach to analyse the emergence of collaboration and competition in the biotechnology sector. After drawing a sample of dedicated biotech firms in the early 1990s, they have mapped out the evolution of the network structures in this emerging industry, and have subsequently examined and explained their effects on organizational learning. With their data on collaborative ties (for example, R&D alliances, investment and marketing cooperation) between dedicated biotech firms and their strategic partners (for example, other dedicated biotech firms, venture capitalists, universities, pharmaceutical firms), Powell and colleagues have tested several hypotheses concerning the relationships between R&D alliances, experiences with inter-firm relationship management, network positions, rates of growth and portfolios of collaborative activities. The first hypothesis, which links a firm's current number of R&D alliances and collaborative experience to future non-R&D ties and any diversity of ties, is confirmed by the data. Similarly, the second hypothesis, which relates the number of R&D alliances, collaborative experience and portfolio diversity to a firm's centrality within a network in the subsequent year, is supported. All three variables have a positive influence on how fast and deep a firm becomes centrally connected in the inter-firm network. The third hypothesis, stipulating that collaborative experience and network centrality have a positive impact on a firm's growth (operationalized in terms of number of employees and stock market performance) is strongly supported by the results. Finally, the fourth hypothesis, predicting that centrality positively affects future collaborative R&D activity, was also confirmed by the data; that is, occupying a central position in a network implies that a firm has relatively more opportunities for future collaboration.

The central thesis emerging from the empirical findings of Powell et al. (1996) is that, in many of the high-technology industries, today's networks of inter-firm collaboration are characterized by cycles of mutual learning. A market entry through R&D partnerships offers young biotech firms pathways to access information and ideas as well as opportunities for further collaboration in other areas, which provide additional possibilities to collect and incorporate new knowledge. Collaboration allows the firms to carry out R&D and develop new alternatives, while simultaneously mitigating the costs, risks and problems associated with such an exploration route. An early choice in favour of exploration through collaboration will generate positive feedback firms can also use to enhance their exploitation efforts and refine and extend their existing competencies (March, 1991). The development of experience and diversity in network ties not only infuses the dedicated biotech firms with experiences in managing inter-firm linkages, but external collaboration also helps develop and strengthen internal competencies for evaluating external research and appropriating the new information and resources. In other words, when they exchange, share and assimilate expertise and experience, these biotech firms continuously enhance their 'absorptive capacity' (Cohen and Levinthal, 1990). In this respect, inter-firm collaboration (and its offspring) is neither a substitute for internal R&D, nor compensation for internal capabilities that are lacking, but external collaboration, as Powell et al. (1996) emphasize, allows firms to enhance all of their competencies.

According to Hargadon and Sutton (1997), the area of innovation theory and management contains a few persistent myths, such as the cult of the lone creative inventor, the instantaneity of the invention, the creation of everything from nothing, the clear break from the past and the linearity of the invention into a marketable product. In today's world there are, however, no solitary geniuses, no immaculate innovations, no glorious eureka moments. The idea that new inventions are built from scratch and the assumption that the development between idea and marketable product is a linear process are also myths. The 'new new thing', regarded as something to be developed to aspire for the future, is often a recombination of existing components in a process that involves adopting and adapting solutions. There is no such thing as an 'immaculate innovation', born of sheer inspiration and untouched by previous inventions, created by extraordinary people in a flash of genius. Instead, innovators like Thomas Edison or James Dyson put inventions together from what they already knew and recombined existing ideas and practices from other industries and innovators. Innovation requires various kinds of input, skills and combinative capabilities. Edison, for example, did not owe his success to his ability to build something from nothing, but rather to his ability to exploit his network, and borrow the ideas of others and incorporate and recombine them in his breakthrough innovations. Edison was not a lone creative genius, but he depended on the close collaboration of his team in his own lab, and extraordinary innovations are often the result of recombinant invention, and innovation is the result of synthesizing and bridging ideas from different domains. Most of Edison's innovations were improvements on existing products and he drew on the existing ideas of other people while working on similar problems in other industries.

The pursuit of innovation, however, involves bringing together previously disparate people, ideas and objects, and inventions emerge in the interactions of the groups involved. As Hargadon (2003) argues convincingly, there is an inherent paradox in the innovation process: on the one hand, innovators need wide-ranging ties from distant environments to generate the sketchy innovative ideas, while, on the other hand, they also need the backing of solid and determined partners and mobilize support for their emerging innovations. In the words of Hargadon (2003, p. 17):

> What set Edison's laboratory apart was not the ability to shut itself off from the rest of the world, to create something from nothing, to think outside the box. Exactly the opposite: It was the ability to *connect* that made the lab so innovative. If Edison ignored anything, it was the belief that innovation was about the solitary pursuit of invention. Edison was able to continuously innovate because he knew how to exploit the networked landscape of his time.

Edison is a broker par excellence: well-positioned between two otherwise disconnected groups, the broker seeks to combine existing but previously distant objects, ideas and people in new ways, building new networks between and around these innovative (re)combinations. For Hargadon

(2003), technology or knowledge brokering includes both bridging old and small worlds effectively and building new worlds from the best pieces of the old ones. These knowledge brokers have access to a broader range of ideas and span multiple industries and technology domains and innovate by putting the various ingredients together into a new solution.

Hargadon and Sutton (1997) have looked at the importance of brokering in product design companies, such as IDEO and Design Continuum. These 'invention factories' seek to create and make both technically feasible and commercially viable innovations for their customers. Their business is 'innovation on demand' and in order to make these new products, concepts and solutions little creativity is needed. Like Edison's laboratory of the past, these product design companies act as brokers, capitalizing success-fully on their connections with many different industries that may not otherwise be connected. As true (technology) brokers, they clearly benefit from their central position and from gaps in the information flow between subgroups in a larger network, and they fill these gaps by combining tech-nologies from within and outside their clients' industry into new solutions. They bring together information flows and design solutions in one area that are potentially valuable in others. Technology brokering furthermore depends on organizational memory, which allows a company to acquire, retain and retrieve new combinations of information for possible use in future design projects. The process of technology brokering is visible not only at the intermediate level (between firms and between sectors), but also at the micro level (among professionals, teams and divisions). Within firms product developers and designers see each other and their larger community as a valuable clearing house for generating and selecting solutions, drawing upon the ideas, tools and artefacts of themselves, their colleagues and the joint input and feedback at Monday morning meetings and informal lunches. Thus, networks appear to be crucial to knowledge brokering. New combinations, an important form of innovation, often involve a combination of outside knowledge with inside competences, which means that the brokering role provided by network ties plays a pivotal role in innovations. Consequently, in the next section we focus on the network contribution to innovation.

NETWORKS AND INNOVATION

In innovative entrepreneurship literature there is a clear bias in favour of heroic entrepreneurs breaking away from existing practices and introduc-ing radically new products and services. This picture does not apply to most entrepreneurs, however, because to a large extent they maintain the status quo by imitating established ideas and practices and/or marketing incremental innovations. Relevant earlier experience is a crucial variable in this respect: actors with extensive experience in an industry are less likely to be innovative than those with limited experience. Unfamiliarity with or even indifference to industry routines and norms may allow outsiders to break away from the cognitive and institutional constraints facing incumbents. Another myth is that these heroic entrepreneurs predominantly act individually and selfishly. Most entrepreneurial activities, even those of solo entrepreneurs, are embedded in ongoing networks of social relationships (Granovetter, 1985). Uzzi (1997) argues that the social and economic embeddedness of entrepreneurs is a two-edged sword, ranging from underembedded (dominated by strong profit orientation, individualism and arm's length relationships) to overembedded networks (characterized by knowledge sharing and trust-based relationships).

Young entrepreneurial ventures often lack the resources that are needed to survive and grow. This 'liability of newness' (Stinchcombe, 1965) results from the high levels of uncertainty and vulnerability surrounding new ventures and their future prospects, which make potential resource providers hesitant to commit resources to start-up firms. In addressing the question as to how new ventures can overcome the problems associated with low levels of legitimacy, Stuart et al. (1999) suggest that inter-organizational exchange relationships can act as endorsements that influence the perceived quality of young organizations when other indicators are unavailable. Inter-organizational collaboration can also be a locus for innovation (Powell et al., 1996). Rather than obtaining new information through the market place (for example, buying information, hiring consultants and so on) or organizing the innovation process internally through the corporate hierarchy (for example, indigenous R&D departments), the source of new information and ideas in knowledge-intensive industries is explored and exploited collectively by inter-firm partnerships and mutual learning. In the biotechnology sector, for example, a complex and rapidly expanding sector that is characterized by a widely dispersed knowledge base, collaboration stems from the actors' need to explore new fields and gain access to specific knowledge and resources. At a later stage, after having learned the tricks and the trade of inter-organizational collaboration and learning with various partners, they can widen and deepen their competencies and knowledge base (and possibly develop new products).

The search process in which entrepreneurs engage to find information, resources and partners within their industrial community consists of a matching process in which participants use a combined set of categories to identify a set of potential participants and relational criteria to establish the trustworthiness of the participants, using emotional criteria, as generated

in face-to-face interactions, to decide whether they should further pursue
a relationship (Nohria, 1992). One entrepreneur sees new venture creation,
like innovation, as a case of brokering:

> a high-technology venture is like a jigsaw puzzle. Each of the pieces is unique
> and must fit together perfectly if you want the venture to be a success. So the
> chase in which everybody is involved – be it the entrepreneur, the venture capi-
> talist, the management candidate or whoever else is in the game – is the search
> for those perfect 'matches' that will help put the puzzle together. (Nohria, 1992,
> p. 243)

The Importance of Weak External Ties and Structural Holes

New technology firms are extremely risky, as they pursue to commercialize
unproven technologies that require substantial investments while future
revenues are highly uncertain. Since the quality of these ventures often
cannot be observed directly, for example from a proven patenting track
record, resource holders must assess the value of a young company by
looking at the attributes of its exchange partners. There are three mechanisms that explain why the social structure of business relationships can
significantly affect the perceptions of the quality (and hence value) of new
ventures: reciprocal relationships, quality assessments and reliability. In
their study involving a sample of 301 young biotech firms, Stuart et al.
(1999) demonstrate that the prominence of the exchange partners of these
firms has a significant positive impact on their subsequent performance.

The first mechanism affecting the perceived quality of a new venture
quality that are affected stresses the reciprocal nature of exchange relationships. Because ties have a reciprocal impact on the reputation of actors,
reputable actors run the risk of damaging their reputation when engaging
in relationships with low quality ventures. The second mechanism involves
the ability of reputable actors to make valid assessments in conditions of
high uncertainty. Prominent third parties are assumed to have superior
expertise at the due diligence process, which implies that a decision to
transact with a new venture reflects an endorsement of sufficient quality
with regard to the start-up organization. The third mechanism through
which third party affiliations influence the perceived quality of new ventures concerns the signalling effect of these affiliations. Assuming that
reputable partners will eschew relationships with low quality ventures and
that entering into a relationship with reputable partners draws relatively
more attention to a new venture, these exchange relationships signal the
reliability and trustworthiness of the young firm to a wide audience.

The empirical analysis focuses on three types of inter-firm collaborations: R&D alliances marketing alliances and product development

alliances. Hypotheses are tested that relate the prominence of strategic alliance partners, outside investors and the investment bank of young companies to higher performance in terms of time-to-IPO and market value at the time of an initial public offering (IPO) (investment bank prominence is measured by taking a prestige ranking for the banks concerned). The prominence of alliance partners and outside investors is measured in terms of their commercial and technological stature. The former refers to actor centrality in the strategic alliance network, while the latter involves the centrality score of the affiliation partner in the biotechnology patent citation network, which consists of all patent citations among biotech firms.

Controlling for firm differences and environmental conditions, the empirical analyses show that new firms with prominent exchange partners go public faster and receive significantly higher valuations when they do. That this is especially true for new firms about which there was high uncertainty is an indication that the positive effects of these affiliations is not only due to access to valuable resources, but also to a transfer of status from prominent partners to new firms. Further analyses indicate that ventures that exchange with prominent partners are able to do so across all types of alliances, which indicates that the endorsements involved have a positive impact on future opportunities to collaborate with prominent partners.

The central question posed by Ruef (2002) has to do with the factors that enable or constrain entrepreneurs (or entrepreneurial teams) to engage in creative action, measured by the number of patent and trademark applications and subjective perceptions about innovations by the entrepreneurs themselves. Ruef (2002) investigates the impact of the social networks of entrepreneurs on their creative actions. These social relationships, including external contacts (for example, with investors, customers, knowledge centres and so on) and internal ties (for example, composition of teams, the structure and the nature of intra-firm networks) can have both a positive and negative effect on innovativeness. In Ruef's theoretical framework the capacity for creative action is seen as a function of three underlying structural and cultural mechanisms: (1) accessing diverse sources of information and obtaining non-redundant information from social networks; (2) avoiding pressures to conform; and (3) sustaining trust with others who are told about a potential innovation in developing new – and potentially profitable – innovations. The intensity, content and diversity of the social ties is specified and operationalized in the following ways:

● strong ties: discussions with relatives and friends;
● weak ties: discussions with business associates, such as customers and suppliers;

● ties directed towards discourse: discussions in the general media or specialized press.

Using a sample of 766 single and multi-member teams that all attempted to start business ventures, Ruef examined how the social network ties and enculturation of entrepreneurs affect their level of innovative activity. His empirical results provide strong support for the expectation that entrepreneurs relying on weak ties (acquaintances) as sources of ideas are more innovative than those with strong ties (family and friends), since weak ties offer new information (echoing Granovetter, 1973) and present less pressure for social conformity. His results also demonstrate the value of network diversity. Entrepreneurs with heterogeneous networks are significantly more likely to engage in innovative behaviour than those with homogeneous networks. This suggests that diversity combines the feedback benefits of social ties with the lack of pressure to conform associated with directed ties. Next, entrepreneurs with ties that are directed at the concrete activities of other actors are found to be more innovative and those with ties directed to the abstract discussion of ideas in expert discourse (for example, the business press) to be less innovative than entrepreneurs relying on weak ties. This is explained by the notion that the former present ready to implement solutions, while the latter only offer general ideas that require adaptation to the specific context, thereby fostering creativity and innovation.

Because many ventures are set up by entrepreneurial teams, Ruef has looked into the role of team structure and internal ties. He found that team size and role diversity among team members had a positive affect on innovation efforts, but when limiting the sample to team start-ups, these variables were insignificant, which indicates that teams are more innovative than solo entrepreneurs, as they tap into a larger and more diverse pool of knowledge, but that this benefit only occurs when moving from single to multi-member teams. Similarly, role diversity may only be beneficial when performed by solo entrepreneurs, but not for heterogeneous teams. Next, teams composed exclusively of relatives, friends or work colleagues (strong ties) were found to be slightly less innovative than those consisting of acquaintances or a mix of relatives, friends and colleagues (weak ties), who in turn were slightly less innovative than teams involving no prior relationships. The differences were, however, not statistically significant, which may be explained by the possibility that once teams are formed which involve people without prior relationships cohesion among group members builds quickly and weak ties become stronger.

In addition to the entrepreneurs' structural embeddedness in social networks, Ruef (2002) also investigates the effect of the cultural embeddedness of entrepreneurs on their innovative behaviour. Cultural embeddedness refers to the level of experience an actor has in a particular task domain, the extent to which that experience is used and the degree to which it involves conventional routines and competences. Entrepreneurs with extensive experience in the industry in which their new venture operates may be less likely to depart from the norms and routines that are prevalent in that industry. Controlling for the age of entrepreneurs, the empirical analyses show that both in the whole sample and in the sub-sample of multi-member teams the (average) number of years of industry experience significantly decreases the likelihood that entrepreneurs perceive themselves as innovators and that they apply for patents or trademarks.

The overall development of more diverse network ties, higher levels of absorptive capacity and better internal capabilities allows firms to increase their centrality in the collaboration network. This inter-organizational network, however, also reflects the nature and intensity of competition in a given sector. The strategic positioning, manoeuvring and partnering of these biotech firms not only shape their reputation and status among peers, but the degree of connectedness may provide a lever to access more and better knowledge and attract additional partners. This enhanced centrality and visibility as a respectable partner implies access to the core of the network in terms of better access to critical resources and information on emerging opportunities. A dynamic feedback process involving organizational learning is set in motion, in which centrally positioned firms are provided with better opportunities and better strategic partners to further and benefit from R&D, overall collaboration, additional ideas and knowledge, and spillovers in other areas. Alternatively, firms with a less central position in the network or without collaborative relationships face a so-called 'liability of unconnectedness', which inhibits access to valuable knowledge and strategic partners (Powell et al., 1996, p. 143).

The Importance of Strong External Ties

Entrepreneurs try to compensate a shortage of human and financial capital by resorting to their networks. Close support networks, based on strong ties (for example, spouse, family) may provide a founder/owner with the resources they owe is lacking (Bruederl and Preisendoerfer, 1998). Although founders with a broad network may simply have more opportunities to raise start-up capital, active help from spouse on life partner and particular support from the family network are vital to increase the chances of success and provide stability to the new firm in its early stages. Yli-Renko et al. (2001) have examined how the social capital embedded in relationships between young technology-based firms and their single largest customer affects knowledge acquisition and how this knowledge mediates the relationship between social capital and knowledge exploitation for competitive advantage. Using a sample of 180 young technology-based firms in the UK, the first set of hypotheses relates three aspects of social capital (social interaction, relationship quality and customer network ties) embedded in the firms' relationships with their key customer (highest proportion of sales revenue) to the acquisition of external business knowledge. A second set of hypotheses examines how this knowledge acquisition relates to knowledge exploitation in terms of new product development, enhanced technological distinctiveness and reductions in sales costs.

The empirical findings of the above-mentioned study support the prediction that social interaction and customer network ties significantly increase knowledge acquisition by new technology-based firms, while, in contrast to expectations, the quality of the relationships was found to have a significant negative effect on knowledge acquisition. Higher levels of social interaction that involve intensive and frequent interactions increase knowledge acquisition by means of a more intense information exchange, an increased willingness and ability to share knowledge and a better ability on the part of firms to recognize and evaluate knowledge. Customer network ties, which refers to the ability of a key customer to provide the focal firm with introductions to a broader set of customers, enhances knowledge acquisition, as it offers technology-based firms access to a wider pool of knowledge embedded in indirect ties, making it possible to build knowledge integration skills. Finally, the finding that the quality of relationships decreases knowledge acquisition may be explained by the possibility that although it may lower monitoring costs and speed up exchange processes, it does not increase the amount of external knowledge acquisition.

After having looked at the relationship between social capital, that is, the linkages of young technology-based firms with their key customers and knowledge acquisition, Yli-Renko et al. (2001) analyse how this knowledge acquisition relates to knowledge exploitation aimed at gaining a competitive advantage. They find that knowledge acquisition, measured by four statements asking respondents to what extent they obtain business knowledge from their key customer, has a significant positive relationship with the number of new product introductions and the technological distinctiveness of young technology-based firms. The former is measured by estimates regarding new products resulting specifically from the key customer relationship, while the latter is measured by three statements regarding the extent to which the firm's technology is a source of competitive advantage. Interestingly, the observation that key customer ties improve a firm's technological distinctiveness is at odds with other studies arguing that relying too much on a single customer may reduce the creativity and innovation of young ventures. Finally, the results demonstrate that knowledge acquisition has a significant negative relationship to the sales cost levels of young technology-based firms. This indicates that knowledge acquired from key customers allows these firms to improve the efficiency of their overall operations. Knowledge gained from a specific collaboration is consequently applied effectively in other areas to raise the firms' effectiveness in a variety of domains.

In contrast to many other studies that explain differences in capabilities among firms by taking an atomistic view in which firms are assumed to act alone and produce their capabilities internally, McEvily and Zaheer (1999) take an embeddedness-oriented perspective by looking at the external sources of competencies. They try to explain the heterogeneity in a firm's capabilities by referring to the differences in its network ties. Using a stratified random sample of 227 manufacturers located in the Midwest of the USA, the study specifically tests hypotheses regarding the relationship between bridging ties, participation in regional institutions and the acquisition of competitive capabilities by firms operating within the same geographical cluster. It is expected that firms located in these clusters benefit from the high levels of trust embedded in those tight-knit communities, as well as from the knowledge sharing that enhances organizational learning by providing access to new information. Since firms maintain idiosyncratic patterns of social network ties, they may be differentially exposed to new information and opportunities arising in these clusters. Bridging ties refer to relationships that link a focal firm to contacts in economic, professional and social circles that are not otherwise accessible to the firm.

To test these alternative explanations, McKevily and Zaheer (1999) relate structural holes (Burt) and tie strength (Granovetter) measures in a firm's advice networks (the five most important sources of advice) to the acquisition of three competitive capabilities that are specific to the job shop manufacturing industry: pollution prevention, quality management and competitive scanning. Controlling for firm size and age, the hypothesis that structural holes in the advice network (measured in terms of its density) have a positive effect on the acquisition of capabilities is strongly supported. By contrast, weak ties, operationalized in terms of infrequency of interaction with the advice network and the geographic dispersion of these contacts, turn out to be insignificantly related to the acquisition of capabilities. Although geographic dispersion is significantly related to one of the three capabilities, the general results confirm the argument that non-redundant networks leverage organizational performance. In addition to bridging ties, the acquisition of competitive capabilities may also be enhanced by ties to regional support institutions. Given the intermediary role of these institutions within networks, they facilitate access to a varied pool of information and knowledge at low cost to participating firms. This access allows member firms to acquire new capabilities and extend existing ones,. A three-item scale capturing the use of available services measured participation in regional institutions. The findings of McKevily and Zaheer (1999) to a large extent confirm the hypothesis that ties to regional institutions enhance capability acquisition. In addition, empirical evidence supports the expectation that structural holes in a firm's advice network are negatively related to participation in regional institutions. This suggests that firms with networks that are rich in information are aware of their value and are consequently hesitant to engage in regional institutions, as this may involve the risk of proprietary information leaking to other firms in the cluster.

The Contingency Argument to Reconcile Conflicting Results

The contingency argument supposes that the need to innovate and engage in networking activities varies across sectors and depends on the ambitions, experience and tasks of the entrepreneur, and the phase in which where his or her company and industry finds itself. In stable and well-organized sectors the networking activities of owner-entrepreneurs aimed at collecting information and mobilizing resources seem to be limited (Chell and Baines, 2000; O'Donnell, 2004). This may be due to the fact that those owner-entrepreneurs may not have a strong need to search for new knowledge through old and new, and strong and weak ties (the overall level of innovativeness and competition are not that high). They may also be inward looking and prefer to run their firm as their empire (the corporation as a fortress) almost by themselves, and they may not have the time or social skills needed for strategic networking. Chell and Baines (2000) have emphasized that it is especially in knowledge-intensive industries that most entrepreneurs force themselves (or are forced by others) to be pro-active and to invest time and energy in their networking in order to grow. The ambition to innovate and grow is then materialized through the active pursuit of new opportunities and the mobilization of additional valuable resources through network contacts, in many cases more specifically through external and weak network ties. Chell and Baines (2000) have also tried to analyse the role of social networks at critical junctures in the career path of owner-founders or the life cycle of their companies. In the case of so-called critical incidents in the personal development of entrepreneurs and in the evolution of their firms, social networks are important and they are functional in the sense that they put entrepreneurs and their firm back on track. Unfortunately, Chell and Baines are unable to specify whether at such a turning point in either a person's or a firm's development strong or weak ties, and internal or external networks are relevant and decisive.

Another contingency is time or, more particularly, the phase of growth of a start-up. On the basis of a literature review, Hite and Hesterly (2001) argue that in the emergence phase start-up firms benefit most from strong ties. In that phase they need a 'friend's favour' in terms of being provided with access to resources. The advantages of weak ties and structural holes only become relevant later on in the early growth stage, when start-ups have to explore new markets or products and expand their network to include weak ties as well. The argument involving the dependence on strong ties has to do with the high level of uncertainty with which the new venture is faced. Strong ties are willing to provide the resources despite the uncertainty, while weak ties tend not to take the risk associated with the uncertain future of a start-up.

Furthermore, in the early growth phase it is necessary to develop a more diverse network in which weak ties may appear to be crucial in terms of discovering structural holes, which are important in gaining access to new resource providers to fuel further growth. Thus, Hite and Hesterly (2001) propose that network benefits develop from the exploitation of strong ties to the exploration of weak ties. The argument by Hite and Hesterly (2001) concerning the growing importance of weak ties as a venture evolves from emergence to early growth emphasizes the need to find structural holes. Structural holes and the role of weak ties are related to the discovery of information about new growth areas. This information, and consequently weak ties, may be important in terms of spotting new opportunities. Of course this search process will benefit from weak ties, but it remains to be seen whether the weak tie benefit is not much larger in the emergence phase (Elfring and Hulsink, 2007). In that phase, when the entrepreneur, the firm and the portfolio of activities have not yet been proven and lack a track record, there is a great need for information and advice about the products and the business model to be selected.

Rowley et al. (2000) also adopt a contingency-oriented perspective to explore the conditions under which sparse (or dense) and strong (or weak) ties are positively related to firm performance, by specifying a particular industry context. They expect that the relationship between embeddedness and firm performance is moderated by the uncertainty and level of innovation in the environment: 'strong and weak ties are beneficial to firms but under different conditions for different purposes and at different times' (Rowley et al., 2000, p. 383). In their study on inter-firm collaboration and its influence on performance, Rowley et al. (2000) address the question as to how firms are embedded in networks of alliances in their particular industry, in this case the dynamic and innovative semiconductor industry or the relatively stable and well-organized steel sector.

Furthermore, they investigate structural and relational embeddedness at the same time, basically to show that these are no independent constructs, but that the interaction between them is an important variable. Relational embeddedness refers to the strength of relationships and the assets rooted in these ties. Strong ties are argued to provide trust-based governance and fine-grained information transfer due to a frequent interaction between relatively similar actors. Weak ties, on the other hand, provide access to new information, as they usually connect actors with different backgrounds. Structural embeddedness concerns the pattern of relationships and the presence or absence of ties between pairs of actors. Sparse networks rich in structural holes between disconnected actors are argued to enhance access to new information, while cohesive networks with high levels of interconnectedness are expected to encourage cooperative behaviour between actors in the network.

Drawing on two datasets involving horizontal strategic alliances in the semiconductor and steel industries, hypotheses are tested regarding the effects of relational and structural embeddedness, as well as the interaction between the two, on firm performance in both industries. Data is collected for the period 1990–7 and collaboration is categorized as either consisting of weak ties, operationalized as alliances involving technology licensing or marketing agreements, or of strong ties that involve non-equity R&D collaboration, joint ventures or equity alliances. The empirical findings confirm the hypotheses that weak tie collaboration has a significant positive relationship with firm performance (return on assets) in the semiconductor industry, whereas strong ties significantly increase the performance of collaborators in the steel industry. However, the hypothesis that strong ties have a significant negative relationship to firm performance in the semiconductor industry is not supported. These findings indicate that in environments that are characterized by high degrees of uncertainty and that demand more exploration on the part of firms, weak ties are more valuable due to their informational advantages. Empirical evidence with regard to the value of networks that are rich in structural holes *vis-à-vis* network cohesion suggests that industry context again plays an important role. A significant positive relationship between firm performance and network density is found in the steel industry, which suggests that firms in environments that are characterized by a high degree of stability and exploitation benefit more from dense networks.

On the basis of the independent tests of relational and structural embeddedness on firm performance in both industries, Rowley et al. (2000) argue that strong ties and dense networks provide firms with alternative governance mechanisms, which when combined provide little additional benefit. To test this hypothesis an interaction variable is introduced to the model that captures the relationships between the two constructs. The findings indeed confirm the prediction that maintaining strong ties when a firm's contacts are already highly connected has a significant negative relationship ($p < 0.10$) with firm performance, both in the combined sample and in the two separate samples. This suggests that the roles that interconnectedness and tie strength play in firm performance are highly interdependent.

Combining Strong/Weak Tie Contributions and/or Internal/External Network Sources

In his longitudinal study on the emergence of inter-organizational alliances of learning in the international chemicals industry Ahuja (2000) relates three different aspects of a firm's network of horizontal technological alliances to the firm's subsequent innovation output, as measured in terms of the number of patents in a given year: direct ties (access to resource and information), indirect ties (sources of information) and structural holes (disconnections between a firm's partners may expand the diversity of information). Ahuja (2000) mentions two primary benefits of inter-firm technological collaboration: resource sharing (sharing tacit knowledge, skills and physical assets) and knowledge spillovers (transmission of codified information in terms of news about technological breakthroughs, new insights into problems or failed approaches).

Three dimensions of a firm's alliance network that are important drivers of innovation are the number of direct ties, the number of indirect ties and the number of structural holes. Firstly, the number of direct ties can have a positive impact on innovative output by providing firms with enhanced knowledge sharing abilities, complementary skills and assets from different firms, and economies of scale, since larger projects significantly generate more knowledge than smaller projects. Secondly, a firm's innovative output may not only be stimulated by benefits provided through their direct partners, but also be increased by the knowledge spillovers from their partners' partners. These indirect ties increase the amount of new information received by firms on promising new opportunities and enhance their ability to identify partners that have valuable information concerning specific problem areas. Finally, structural holes may both increase and reduce a firm's innovative output. From a knowledge spillover point of view, structural holes increase access to non-redundant information. From a resource sharing perspective, structural holes imply a lack of trust building and a risk of opportunistic behaviour that inhibit cooperation and resource sharing.

The hypotheses are tested on a longitudinal dataset comprising the linkage and patenting activities of 97 leading firms from the chemicals industry in Western Europe, Japan and the USA between 1981 and 1991. Control variables include a firm's R&D expenditures, size, diversification of sales, strategic focus, international research presence, profitability and liquidity, and the technological distance between the firm and its partners. Empirical results confirm the predictions that the number of direct and indirect ties has a significant positive relationship to innovation output. Furthermore, introducing an interaction variable reveals that the value of indirect ties is inversely related to a firm's number of direct ties. Finally, the number of structural holes is found to have a significant negative relationship to innovation output.

The finding that indirect ties have a positive impact on innovation suggests that these ties provide firms with a mechanism of knowledge spillovers that contributes to innovation. Given the low costs of maintaining indirect ties, it may therefore seem optimal for firms to build large networks of indirect ties. However, three factors need to be considered before doing so. Firstly, the benefits of direct ties (resource sharing and knowledge spillover) are different than those provided by indirect ties (knowledge spillovers only). The degree to which substitution is possible is therefore limited. Secondly, even when the kind of benefits that are being provided are the same, their magnitude may vary significantly between the two types of ties. The benefits of direct ties are significantly larger than those provided by indirect ties, as the latter often also involve competitors that may appropriate the same benefits. Thirdly, having a large number of direct ties may involve a limited ability on the part of a firm to benefit from information provided by its indirect ties, since the information that is being exchanged also reaches the firm's direct ties.

Recently, Burt (2000) has contributed to the debate on the (beneficial or detrimental) effects of a dense network with trust and strong ties (Krackhardt, 1992; Coleman, 1998) versus a sparse network with few redundancies and weak ties (Granovetter, 1973; Burt, 1992) on the performance of entrepreneurial ventures. Alternatively, cohesive networks act as a defence against opportunism and structural holes and weak tie networks help prevent lock-in, conservatism and rigidity. While structural holes theory offers firms informational and control advantages (diversity, strategic positioning), network closure theory highlights benefits in exchanging trustworthy information and tacit knowledge, joint problem solving and collective monitoring. Burt (2000, p. 410) tries to reconcile the two perspectives: 'although brokerage across structural holes is the source of added value, closure can be critical to realising the value buried in the holes'. Although structural holes may provide an entrepreneur or manager with timely access to and information about new opportunities, cohesive ties among players whose cooperation is also needed in order to exploit those opportunities is also an essential component of success. To find a balance between safety and adaptability (both bonding and bridging are needed to generate and sustain innovation) a mixture of a union and disunion strategy is required, depending on the institutional context and the stage of the industry's life cycle (Baker and Obstfeld, 1999).

An attempt to look at bridging the contribution of internal and external networks to firm performance was made by Menon and Pfeffer (2003), who try to analyse the ways in which managers value knowledge from internal and external sources. While most theories take favouritism towards insiders into account, Menon and Pfeffer (2003) found that a preference in favour of knowledge obtained from outsiders was also prevalent. In some situations managers may prefer internal knowledge, because they tend to overemphasize readily available knowledge and can limit their search to internally available or doable options; in existing literature this is described by concepts like as in-group favouritism, the 'not-invented here' syndrome and out-group derogation. Menon and Pfeffer (2003) have demonstrated that managers value external knowledge more highly than internal knowledge. In fact, the companies in their small sample were almost unresponsive to internal knowledge, while being receptive when it came to ideas and technologies that originated their company (the 'invented elsewhere' syndrome, exhibiting a favouritism to out-group knowledge and overemphasizing the importance of external knowledge (in-group denigration)).

Thus, less accessible and sparser external knowledge became relatively overvalued and overused, compared to accessible rich internal knowledge, from which value could have been captured more easily. Menon and Pfeffer (2003) try to explain this preference for outsider knowledge by referring to the contrasting status implications of learning from internal versus external competitors and to the relative availability of knowledge (internal knowledge is readily available but subject to greater scrutiny, while external knowledge is more special and unique despite being sparse). In short, strong market competition seemed to make knowledge from external sources more valuable for managers than ideas and information that are generated internally, and when the external knowledge was internalized, the managers saw it as less valuable.

CONCLUSION

External network ties, in combination with internal competences, play an important role in the discovery and realization of innovations. However, it is not true that more ties or larger networks are by definition better. A particular mix of strong and weak ties and a particular position in the network structure is preferable when it comes to discovering and realizing innovations. Much of the debate on the importance of social networking for innovation for (young and small) firms has to do with the question which ties matter when. The central aim of this chapter has been to review existing literature on the various dimensions of networks and examine how these different network dimensions may contribute to innovation. Although we can draw some conclusions about particular network benefits, many issues about the most 'optimal' network with regard to innovation remain unresolved. Contingencies play an important role, and most researchers have agreed that the purpose and circumstances have a major impact on the particular role network ties can play.

What do we know? The higher the level of uncertainty and the greater the need to search for the exact nature of an innovation, the more important new information is. Thus, weak ties and structural holes will play a crucial beneficial role in these kinds of circumstances, which are most likely to be relevant to radical innovations and in the discovery phase. In the opposite situation involving limited uncertainty, which is found in the case of incremental innovations and situations involving the realization of an innovation, strong ties and dense networks appear to be more beneficial. In both cases the object is not to have only strong or weak ties, and there will always be a mixture, although in these more clear-cut circumstances we refer to the dominant network effect. In the other cases in the matrix it is not entirely clear from the literature which mixture is the most beneficial.

REFERENCES

Ahuja, G. (2000), 'The duality of collaboration: inducements and opportunities in the formation of inter-firm linkages', *Strategic Management Journal*, **21**, 317–43.
Baker, W.E. and D. Obstfeld (1999), 'Social capital by design: structures, strategies and institutional context', in R.Th.A.J. Leenders and S.M. Gabbay (eds), *Corporate Social Capital and Liability*, Boston, MA: Kluwer Academic Publishers, pp. 88–105.
Bruederl, J. and P. Preisendorfer (1998), 'Network support and the business of newly founded businesses', *Small Business Economics* **10**, 213–25.
Burt, R.S. (1992), *Structural Holes: The Social Structure of Competition*, Cambridge, MA: Harvard University Press.
Burt, R.S. (2000), 'The network structure of social capital', *Research in Organizational Behaviour*, **22**, 345–423.
Chell, E. and S. Baines (2000), 'Networking, entrepreneurship and microbusiness behaviour,' *Entrepreneurship & Regional Development*, **12**, 195–215.

Cohen, W.M. and D.A. Levinthal (1990), 'Absorptive capacity: a new perspective on learning and innovation,' *Administrative Science Quarterly*, **35**, 128–52.

Coleman, J.S. (1988), 'Social capital in the creation of human capital', *American Journal of Sociology*, **94**, S95–S120.

Dosi, G. (1988), 'Sources, procedures, and microeconomic effects of innovation', *Journal of Economic Literature*, **26**, 1120–71.

Elfring, T. and W. Hulsink (2007), 'Networking by entrepreneurs: patterns of tie formation for emerging organizations', *Organization Studies*, **28** (12), 1849–72.

Floyd S.W and B. Wooldridge (1999), 'Knowledge creation and social networks in corporate entrepreneurship: the renewal of organizational capability', *Entrepreneurship Theory & Practice*, **23** (3), 123–43.

Gabbay, S.M. and R.Th.A.J. Leenders (1999), 'Corporate social capital: the structure of advantage and disadvantage', in R.Th.A.J. Leenders and S.M. Gabbay (eds), *Corporate Social Capital and Liability*, Boston, MA: Kluwer Academic Publishers, pp. 1–14.

Gargiulo, M. and M. Benassi (1999), 'The dark side of social capital', in R.Th.A.J. Leenders and S.M. Gabbay (eds), *Corporate Social Capital and Liability*, Boston, MA: Kluwer Academic Publishers, pp. 298–322.

Granovetter, M. (1985), 'Economic action and social structure: the problem of embeddedness', *American Journal of Sociology*, **91**, 481–510.

Granovetter, M.S. (1973), 'The strength of weak ties', *American Journal of Sociology*, **78**, 1360–80.

Hargadon, A. (1998), 'Firms as knowledge brokers', *California Management Review*, **40**, 209–27.

Hargadon, A. (2003), *How Breakthroughs Happen? The Surprising Truth About How Companies Innovate*, Cambridge, MA: Harvard Business School Press.

Hargadon, A. and R.I Sutton (1997), 'Technology brokering and innovation in a product development firm', *Administrative Science Quarterly*, **42**, 716–49.

Hite, J.M. (2003), 'Patterns of multidimensionality among embedded network ties: a typology of relational embeddedness in emerging entrepreneurial firms', *Strategic Organization*, **1**, 9–49.

Hite, J.M. and W.S. Hesterly (2001), 'The evolution of firm networks: from emergence to early growth of the firm', *Strategic Management Journal*, **22**, 275–86.

Krackhardt, D. (1992), 'The strength of strong ties: the importance of *Philos* in organizations', in N. Nohria and R.G. Eccles (eds), *Networks and organizations: Structure, Form and Action*, Cambridge, MA: Harvard Business School Press, pp. 216–39.

Lee, C., K. Lee and J.M. Pennings (2001), 'Internal capabilities, external networks, and performance: a study on technology-based ventures', *Strategic Management Journal*, **22**, 615–40.

Leenders, R.Th.A.J. and S.M. Gabbay (eds) (1999), *Corporate Social Capital and Liability*, Boston, MA: Kluwer Academic Publishers.

March, J.G. (1991), 'Exploration and exploitation in organizational learning,' *Organization Science*, **2**, 71–87.

McEvily, B. and A. Zaheer (1999), 'Bridging ties: a source of firm heterogeneity in competitive capabilitites', *Strategic Management Journal*, **20**, 1133–56.

Menon, T. and J. Pfeffer (2003), 'Valuing internal vs. external knowledge: explaining the preference for outsiders,' *Management Science*, **49**, 497–513.

Nohria, N. (1992), 'Information and search in the creation of new business ventures: the case of the 128 Venture Group', in N. Nohria and R.G. Eccles (eds),

Networks and Organizations: Structure, Form and Action, Cambridge, MA: Harvard Business School Press, pp. 240–61.

O'Donnell, A. (2004), 'The nature of networking in small firms', *Qualitative Market Research: An International Journal*, **7** (3), 206–17.

Oerlemans, L.A.G., M.T.H. Meeus and F.W.M. Boekema (1998), 'Do networks matter for innovation? The usefulness of the economic networks approach in analysing innovation', *Tijdschrift voor Economische en Sociale Geografie*, **89**, 298–309.

Powell, W.W., K.W. Koput and L. Smith-Doerr (1996), 'Interorganizational collaboration and the locus of innovation: networks of learning in biotechnology', *Administrative Science Quarterly*, **41**, 116–45.

Quinn, J.B., and J.J. Baruch and K.A. Zien (1997), *Innovation Explosion. Using Intellect and Software to Revolutionize Growth Strategies*, New York: Free Press.

Rowley, T., D. Behrens and D. Krackhardt (2000), 'Redundant governance structures: an analysis of structural and relational embeddedness in the steel and semiconductor industries', *Strategic Management Journal*, **21**, 369–86.

Ruef, M. (2002), 'Strong ties, weak ties and islands: structural and cultural predictors or organizational innovation', *Industrial and Corporate Change*, **11**, 427–49.

Stam, W and T. Elfring (2008), 'Entrepreneurial orientation and new venture performance: the moderating role of intra- and extra-industry social capital', *Academy of Management Journal*, **51** (1), 97–111.

Stinchcombe, A. (1965), 'Social structure and organizations', in J.G. March (ed.), *Handbook of Organizations*, Chicago, IL: Rand McNally, pp. 153–93.

Stuart, T.E., H. Hoang and R.C. Hybels (1999), 'Interorganizational endorsements and the performance of entrepreneurial ventures', *Administrative Science Quarterly*, **44**, 315–49.

Uzzi, B. (1997), 'Social structure and competition in inter-firm networks: the paradox of embeddedness', *Administrative Science Quarterly*, **42**, 35–67.

Van De Ven, A.H. (1986), 'Central problems in the management of innovation', *Management Science*, **32**, 590–607.

Weick, K.E. (1979), *The Social Psychology of Organizing*, New York: Random House.

Yli-Renko, H., E. Autio and H.J. Sapienza (2001), 'Social capital, knowledge acquisition, and knowledge exploitation in young technology-based firms', *Strategic Management Journal*, **22**, 587–613.

6. Building a business on open source software

Anthony I. Wasserman

INTRODUCTION

The notions of free and open source software go back to the earliest days of computing, when all software was free and source code was routinely published. In the late 1960s, though, IBM unbundled software from hardware, charging money for the operating system and other software. At about the same time, new software companies arose, building businesses around the licensing and support of software systems, such as database management systems. Software developed in the research community continued to be freely distributed at no charge, even as commercial software grew to a multi-billion dollar industry. Much of the foundation for the Internet was funded by the US Government, with all of the source code freely available.

In 1985 Richard Stallman at MIT put forth the notion of free software based on his personal belief that software should be free. He created the Free Software Foundation (FSF) not just as a technical movement, but also as a social, political and economic movement. In the early 1990s Linus Torvalds, a student in Finland, first developed the Linux operating system, and made it freely available under the GNU General Public License developed by Stallman and the FSF. Linux became extremely popular, especially among hobbyists, who created a large and active community that enhanced Linux, eventually making it sufficiently reliable for widespread commercial use.

Before companies would use Linux or any other free software, they wanted to make sure that there were commercial sources of training and support. In the late 1980s Cygnus Solutions was created to provide such support. Cygnus was able to build a profitable business not by selling software, but by selling services to help people use free software. Cygnus was eventually acquired by RedHat, which has become the leading commercial vendor of Linux software. There was a growing interest in commercialization of open source software which led to the 1998 Open Source Definition

(Perens, 1998). This definition included a set of approved licenses which are managed by a formal organization, the Open Source Initiative (OSI). The OSI is responsible for reviewing and approving open source licenses, as well as promoting open source development and use.

The notion of open source software has three important components. The first is that all of the code and all of the scripts and libraries needed to run the program are made available, without restriction, to anyone who wants access to that code. The second is that the software is licensed under a mechanism that defines appropriate uses for the program and the rules for distributing changes to the source code. Finally, the software is supported by a community of interest, including contributors to the source code. There is little value to software that is released without a community of people to maintain it and test it.

The growth of open source software has transformed the software industry. Many companies now release the source code of the software and make it available under an approved open source license, rather than selling traditional proprietary (closed source) licenses.

THE STATE OF OPEN SOURCE SOFTWARE

Today there is a vast range of open source software available, not just for Linux, but also for Windows and MacOS X. The software includes not only infrastructure software and development tools, but also applications software. At the infrastructure level, it is easy to find highly reliable open source software as web servers, application servers, system management tools and virtualization tools. Among development tools, there are two major integrated development environments, Eclipse and NetBeans, both of which can be used for a wide variety of software development tasks. In addition, both of those development environments are frameworks that support the addition of tools, not necessarily open source, developed by others.

At the application layer, there are not only widely used tools for word processing (for example, OpenOffice), email, (for example, Zimbra) and web browsing (for example, Firefox), but also more specialized applications for accounting, image editing and telephony. More and more of these applications are being developed and supported by new companies, which also provide support, training and the promise of ongoing maintenance. That is a strong contrast with traditional community-based development where there was no such assurance.

There are at least four different kinds of open source projects. The first is a community-based project, started by a small group and developed independently of any organization or company. The developers on these projects often work as volunteers in their free time. The second is a community-based project under the structure of a non-profit organization, such as the Apache Foundation. The Foundation leadership oversees progress of the project and provides some support. Project developers may work as volunteers or may be paid by a company to contribute. The third is a project with both community and commercial aspects. In this case the project may be led by a company, and many of the contributors may be paid by that company to work on the project. However, participation in the project and the group of committers is open to all. The last is a project started by a company that is creating a commercial business around the open source software. In this case the key decisions about the project are made by company management, and all of the developers work for the company, with little opportunity for community volunteers to contribute code.

From a business perspective, there are significant differences among these models. The projects with significant commercial participation often have a more clearly defined project roadmap, a systematic testing process, and mechanisms for both commercial and non-commercial support.

The remainder of this chapter focuses on a variety of business models by which people can build successful businesses on open source software.

TOWARD COMMERCIAL OPPORTUNITIES

The title of this chapter concerns two major options: creating a business that offers services related to open source software, and creating a business that uses open source software to deliver an application or system. In both cases an important prerequisite is that the open source software is of high enough quality that companies will adopt it for their routine and critical business operations. Now that there are many software products that meet that criterion, a large number of possibilities for commercialization arise.

These opportunities are driven, in part, by user unhappiness with traditional software and fee structures. Commercial licenses require the payment of substantial initial fees followed by ongoing support costs. By contrast, open source software has no initial fee and allows an organization to evaluate that software until such time as it is ready to be deployed for commercial purposes. At that time, and only at that time, must the user enter into a commercial agreement with the vendor and pay fees. For most companies, and especially for startups, the savings on the initial license fee is extremely significant.

In addition, companies are looking to save money in general and are beginning to consider open source alternatives as they evaluate different categories of software. Perhaps surprisingly, some users of open source software, especially companies, want to pay and expect to pay for use of that software, as a way to assure that they can obtain service as needed.

These factors, taken together, are transforming the software industry for both vendors and buyers. As one example, established vendors of proprietary closed source products increasingly find themselves competing against open source alternatives. These vendors have responded in several different ways: (1) by offering basic versions of their product at no charge, and hoping to sell support services to those users; (2) by using the offer of the free basic version as a way to build a relationship with users, who may eventually license the paid commercial version, and; (3) acquiring commercial open source companies that enable them to offer an open source alternative and support services to those users who don't want to pay the initial license fees for the proprietary software product.

As another example of industry transformation, software-intensive startups are making extensive use of open source software as building blocks for their products and services. That approach sharply reduces the time, effort and cost needed to bring their product to market, thereby reducing the amount of needed outside investment.

Finally, companies have chosen to release their software under an open source license rather than keeping it closed and distributing it under a proprietary license. For established companies, there are good reasons for choosing to develop and release code under an open source license; Goldman and Gabriel (2005) describe the experience of doing so at Sun Microsystems.

For new companies, the open source strategy allows them to build a user base quickly, beat their competitors on price, and save significantly on sales and marketing expenses. Over time, they develop ways to generate revenue from their software, using one or more of the approaches described in the next section. Unlike community-based open source projects, such as the Apache http server, these commercial open source startups control the development process and effectively own the source code.

In short, the emergence of open source software has affected almost every aspect of the software business, forcing established software vendors to respond to the competitive pressures of open source software, and creating new types of business opportunities that build on open source software.

BUSINESS MODELS USING OPEN SOURCE SOFTWARE

There are many ways by which an individual, a partnership or a company can create a business related to open source software. In some cases it is not necessary for the business to have any particular role in development and maintenance of the code. Weber (2004) has contrasted businesses based on proprietary software with those based on open source software, listed some 'basic business model templates' and described the ways that six different companies have used one or more of these ideas in their businesses.

Fink (2003) described seven different business models in his survey work on open source software, including selling proprietary software on the open source Linux platform and 'open sourcing' legacy proprietary software; these ideas have not been successful and are not included here. Krishnamurthy (2005) identified six different business models that built on open source software, with particular emphasis on selling support services. As we shall see, the marketplace has evolved to present additional options.

In this section we describe many of the most effective ways to create a successful business using open source software, giving specific examples where possible.

Subscription Model

The most widely used business model for open source software is a subscription model, where the user pays a fee for regular updates to the software. In this model there is usually no requirement that a user of the software purchase a subscription, so a user can download software and use it indefinitely at no charge. (RedHat Enterprise Linux is a notable exception to this statement.) The user can manually check for software updates or new releases, install them and use discussion forums for answers to technical problems, again at no charge. In addition, a user can hire consultants and contractors to help with specific issues. Excellent examples of this model are provided by Novell with their SuSE Linux Enterprise Desktop and by RedHat with the JBoss application server.

From a business perspective the subscription model offers some valuable advantages. For a supplier, this current model provides a more predictable revenue flow than is possible with a traditional license model. For customers, it is only necessary to pay for the subscription when they can generate revenue based on the use of that software.

Offering Commercial and Open Source Products

Another approach for a vendor is to offer both open source and commercial products. The commercial products can be licensed in the traditional way, or as an 'on demand' service, and are typically closed source. They can provide significant revenue for the business, which may also offer open source products under other business models or even free of charge.

Among the vendors following this approach are CollabNet, with its Enterprise Edition and the open source Subversion configuration management system. Similarly, JasperSoft offers a commercial JasperServer Business Intelligence suite, as well as an open source community edition of the JasperServer reporting tool.

Krugle offers a non-commercial search mechanism for open source software through their krugle.org site. That site was developed to generate awareness for their commercial enterprise product, aimed at helping companies manage their internal software assets.

Support and Training Model

In addition to selling subscriptions, a common business model involves providing support and training for open source products. Training may come in the form of textbooks and instructional material, such as offering of courses via live training or video.

Textbooks can be a profitable model, but it is important to note that there is a large upfront cost in writing the manuscript, publishing it and making it available for distribution. Nonetheless, there are several publishers, particularly O'Reilly and aPress, who have created a substantial library of books covering various open source software projects.

Some people and organizations have also created small businesses by distributing media, that is, DVDs and CDs, with various open source components. This service is valuable in places where connection speeds are slow and where the charges for transferred data are high. However, this approach does not seem to generate enough revenue or profit to be a sustainable business model.

Training courses can be profitable and can be prepared in relatively little time, especially compared to the time needed to write and publish a book. However, it often takes considerable effort to market the courses to an audience that is large enough to help create a profitable business.

Technical support can be offered as fee-based help or as an ongoing subscription for customers who need someone to call for help with problems and issues that they may have with open source software. Many companies have an IT policy that they will not use any software (open source or not) for which they cannot obtain a support contract with service level agreements appropriate for the criticality of that software. In many cases an open source product may obtain more support contracts when it is acquired by a larger company with extensive geographical coverage, as happened after Oracle's acquisition of Sleepycat Software (BerkeleyDB) and Sun's acquisition of MySQL AB.

In all of these cases it is possible to create a business around one or more software projects without having contributed to the development of that software. This approach is particularly useful when customers need local support, without having to wait for an email reply from a distant organization in a different time zone. Also, since English is so widely used for software and its documentation, it is sometimes difficult to obtain high-quality support in local languages. As software is increasingly localized for these languages, there is a growing need for support in those local languages, making it possible to create a successful business around support and training.

Dual License Model

Another business alternative is to offer open source software under a dual license model, that is, allowing the customer to select the license that will apply for their use of the software. In this approach users can download and freely use the open source software for non-commercial purposes, including evaluation for commercial suitability and development of their products and/or services. When they are ready to offer that software in a product that is licensed or sold to customers, they can then switch licenses, obtaining a commercial license to replace the non-commercial one.

MySQL AB is one company that took this dual license approach. Before they increased their commercial marketing efforts in their last years as an independent company, there were as many as 1000 non-commercial users of MySQL for every commercial one. The revenue from the commercial licenses grew quickly in the past few years and supported the growth of the company which Sun Microsystems acquired in 2008 for $1 billion.

In some cases the software offered in the commercial version offers additional options or features not available in the 'community', that is, open source, version. Users can start out with the open source version, but often find that they need the additional features when they want to use the software in a production environment.

Hosted Service

In a hosted service model a vendor can use open source software to create software that can be offered as a service. There are numerous examples of such a hosted service including web searching, document editing, project management and content management systems. For a software startup, using open source software to build a hosted service is extremely helpful. First, there is no initial cost for software licenses, but more importantly, the startup can focus on the added value that it brings to its service without having to redevelop database management systems or other infrastructure components that will be used to implement their service.

Some of the largest and best known companies have begun by using open source software. Yahoo, for example, built their directory service and other websites on top of a BSD Unix-based open source operating system. Google, as another example, has made extensive use of open source software, particularly the Apache http server, which they have greatly modified to meet their specific needs. Many non-commercial sites also used a combination of open source software to provide their service.

Many of the open source wikis and content management systems employ several different open source components to provide their service, which others then use as the basis for their sites. The Mozilla Foundation created the SpreadFirefox website as a marketing tool for the open source Firefox browser. The website is built using the open source Drupal content management system, which in turn uses the Apache http server, the MySQL database and the PHP scripting language. That site, in turn, serves as a directory for numerous other Firefox-related sites, virtually all of which are built with similar open source tools.

Beyond those examples, open source software is frequently used to create software-as-a-service (SaaS) offerings for which customers may purchase subscriptions. Among the many instances of such SaaS products are the BasecampHQ project management system and the SugarCRM customer relationship management system. BasecampHQ is built with Ruby on Rails, while SugarCRM uses the Apache http server, a relational database management system and PHP. Customers don't pay for the source code, but rather for access to the SaaS application. SugarCRM is particularly interesting, since there is a community open source version, a professional version (where some of the code is not open) and an SaaS version, with the latter two producing revenue for the company.

Advertising Model

While many of the examples cited above present a direct revenue opportunity, for example, from subscriptions or paid services, it is also possible to generate revenue from advertising, as has been amply demonstrated in the market. For example, targeted ads can be displayed on the site where the user accesses an SaaS application. A financial services site could connect to an advertising network, such as Google's AdWords, and deliver ads that are relevant to someone looking for investment opportunities or professional assistance with finance. It is easy to imagine analogous types of ads for open source SaaS applications in other application domains. Of course, this advertising model is already widely used for web applications built on proprietary software, but applies just as well for web applications built on open source software.

An open source-based SaaS application could offer both a paid subscription version and a free version, with advertising displayed on the free version. In this way, the developer of the application is able to monetize all users of the application, using two different approaches, subscriptions and advertising, to do so.

Packaging Model

There are many thousands of open source packages available, many of which, for example, libraries, are only useful in combination with other software. While developers are content to work with individual packages, users are more interested in solutions that may involve combining several different components into a useful grouping. One such example, noted above, is Drupal, which combines a web server, a database management system and the PHP scripting language. The Drupal community has created various modules for such activities as blogging, discussion forums and social networking, along with themes to customize site appearance. Taken together, these pieces provide a simple way to quickly deploy a new site with little or no software development.

Many such packages are becoming available, often with no initial cost. BitRock has sponsored the BitNami site (www.bitnami.org), which has created installation packages for more than 20 different applications, including seven content management systems, three issue tracking systems, two wikis and more. A user can download one of these packages, and the installer will automatically install the various open source components needed to use the chosen application. The availability of such packages greatly simplifies the user's task. Not only is it unnecessary to locate the individual components needed for the application, but the components have been configured to work together for that application.

Along the same lines, OpenLogic has created OpenLogic Exchange, aimed at helping enterprises find and download open source packages. OpenLogic uses a support model as their way of generating revenue from this service. SpikeSource also offers integrated and certified open source packages as part of their Solutions Factory, along with a subscription-based SpikeIgnite program that offers pre-packaged stacks.

Commercial Enhancement

Many open source software projects were not developed with commercial requirements in mind. However, depending on the license associated with the project, it is possible to extend those projects and deliver a commercial product based on enhancements to the underlying software. While most commercial enhancers of open source software contribute the software changes back to the original project, some licenses, such as Berkeley Software Distribution (BSD), do not require that this be done. In that situation the company that makes the commercial enhancement is free to license it on either open source or commercial terms using any business model that seems appropriate.

For example, there are several companies that have enhanced the Postgres database management system. One such project called PowerGres, from SRA, adds high-availability and scalability features to Postgres. Another such product, called Postgres Plus, from EnterpriseDB, offers binary downloads (not source code) of their enhanced version of Postgres. That product is offered at no charge for non-production use, with a commercial license available for production use. Taking an open source program proprietary, that is, 'closing' it, is often seen as going against the spirit of open source software, even if doing so is permitted by the associated license.

Embedding Model

Open source software can also be used as part of a hardware/software product, with the software embedded in the hardware. Because of the licensing requirements on open source software, the product manufacturer must make the (potentially modified) open source software available to anyone who is interested. The manufacturer creates a business based on selling the manufactured product with no intent to generate revenue from the open source software. In this case the manufacturer is simply taking advantage of the open source software to speed development of the embedded product.

There are numerous examples of products built on open source software. One is the TiVo digital video recorder. The Software Development Kit for the TiVo Home Media Engine is available as a project on the SourceForge repository. Another is Amazon.com's Kindle reader device, built on Linux, with the source code for the relevant packages available on Amazon.com's website. Another example is the OpenMoko FreeRunner mobile telephone, in which the NeoSoftwareStack is embedded. That stack includes various open source components, including graphical toolkits, a Java Virtual Machine, the GNU C compiler and many others, all built on a Linux operating system. Finally, most of the routers developed by the Linksys subsidiary of Cisco Systems are based on open source software. The technical support area of the Linksys website contains a list of those routers with a link to the source code for each router, in keeping with the requirements of the General Public License (GPL), under which the code was licensed.

In addition to the multitude of traditional computers on which an open source operating system, for example, Linux or FreeBSD, can be installed, there is also a growing category of devices on which Linux is pre-installed and serves as the de facto operating environment for the device. One example is the Nokia N800/N810 Internet tablet family, for which the Maemo operating system (a Linux variant) serves as the platform. Another, better known, device is the XO Laptop, created by the One Laptop per Child Foundation, which is based on the open source Fedora distribution of Linux, sponsored by RedHat. In both cases the base operating system is augmented by hundreds of additional open source software components, producing a complete operating environment with its own unique characteristics. Different versions of Linux serve as the embedded operating system in many of the new, lightweight 'netbooks', such as the Asus EEE, the MSI Wind and the HP MiniNote, as well as in mobile telephones, including those compliant with the specifications of the LiMo Foundation.

Many open source software components have been developed specifically for use in embedded systems, including versions of Linux optimized for real-time and embedded systems.

Consulting and Integration Strategy

With a consulting strategy, a vendor does not offer open source software directly, but instead helps clients to make strategic decisions and investments related to open source. Consultants charge for their time and services, which may also include installation, integration and customization of software, both open source and proprietary.

Consulting services come in all sizes, ranging from tiny one and two-person operations to the multi-billion dollar IBM Global Services. Some open source developers can make their living by offering consulting services on the open source projects that they have developed. Many of the larger firms, known as system integrators, put together solutions for their business clients. Historically, these solutions have been built almost exclusively on proprietary commercial software; now, however, open source software has become an important component of these solutions. Riehle (2007) describes the system integrator perspective and how their use of open source software improves their business.

For example, a consultant may help with the evaluation of a database management system or a content management system. The selection of the database management system may be followed by application design and schema design, which can be very beneficial to the consulting firm. Other consulting firms, known as industry analysts, don't do any software development at all. Instead, they produce independent reports on technological trends, and may evaluate products in specific categories and/ or organize conferences to report and discuss their findings. For many of these analyst firms, open source software is just one of many lines of practice. Clients of the analyst firms may also receive individual advice, which helps them to make business decisions.

Consulting is a particularly effective business model for individual entrepreneurs, who can work with local companies to help them make the most effective use of open source software. This type of consulting is particularly valuable for small and medium-sized businesses, who lack the resources to use expensive proprietary software or to pay high-priced consulting firms.

In addition to individual product consulting, there is also a need for strategic consulting related to open source software. Many large corporations need advice on how to evaluate, adopt and use open source software, including modification of their IT policies, education about open source licenses and creation of open source contribution policies for their employees. These companies have many years of experience with evaluation and acquisition of proprietary software, but open source is new to them.

Patronage Model

The patronage model involves contribution of people, equipment, time and/or money to open source projects, typically by large corporations. These corporations do not directly receive any revenue from their participation in these projects. However, there are several very good reasons for these companies to contribute resources to open source projects.

First, these companies are often looked upon more favorably because of their contributions. Second, by giving away some of their software, they increase visibility of their own company in the open source community, which may help them to sell their other products and services, including those unrelated to the open source software. Third, as they pay their employees to work on open source projects, their employees become aware of new tools and techniques that may increase their value to the company. Furthermore, their employees work closely with other contributors to open source projects, which helps them to identify people who might make good employees. Thus, the patronage role also serves as a useful recruiting mechanism.

In many cases the extent of the contribution is very substantial. For example, IBM is the major supporter of the Eclipse development environment. Similarly, Sun Microsystems is a leading supporter of OpenOffice, NetBeans and GlassFish. Many companies contribute to the Mozilla Foundation in support of the Firefox browser and Thunderbird email product.

In addition to the paid employees, many individuals also volunteer their time to these large and established products. There are many reasons for doing so, including the sense of belonging to a community, an alternative outlet for creative activities aside from their other activities (possibly including a programming job) and a way to build their own professional credentials, perhaps as an entry on their resumé or a personal contact that could help them to obtain new employment, contracting or consulting work. For an individual, giving time and effort to a project can lead to business opportunities.

Finally, it should be noted that not all of this patronage is entirely benevolent. If a company supports the enhancement of an open source operating system or suite of development tools, its intent may include taking business away from commercial vendors of proprietary operating systems and development tools. Even so, the net result is usually beneficial to those who are interested in having high-quality open source software.

STARTING A NEW OPEN SOURCE BUSINESS

Given this wide range of business models, one could naturally question which of these models present good opportunities for new businesses. There is, of course, no answer that fits everyone. Instead, there are many factors that influence the choice, including not only one's technical and managerial skills and interests, but also available funding and geographical location, which influence market opportunities.

For someone with some technical background, combined with an interest in working with users, it is often easiest to create a business around delivering services on one or more open source projects, particularly in locations outside of North America and Western Europe. Startup costs are low, competition is limited and the service can provide high value to governments, as well as to small and medium-sized businesses. As an adjunct to creating the training and consulting service, it is essential to become a member of the communities for the various open source projects, though not necessarily a source code contributor.

Similarly, it is relatively easy to create a business that applies packaged open source software to the development of websites for small and medium-sized businesses. It is quite straightforward to use the Drupal or Joomla content management systems to create an e-commerce website or a community message center. Both of these small businesses allow the business principal(s) to get started quickly at low cost, and to offer services to customers very quickly.

On the other hand, neither of these small business ideas will lead to a large business opportunity, given their labor-intensive nature. For those opportunities, one must create something unique that can be used by a larger number of people. Both software products and embedded systems fall into this category.

In the realm of software products, the infrastructure and development tools categories are more fully addressed than are applications. One particularly interesting area is games, which can be built using an SaaS model. The area of 'casual gaming' is growing extremely fast, and the most popular games earn large sums of money for their creators and publishers, either through a subscription model or through an ad-supported site. In addition, there are many opportunities involving the development of SaaS applications built on an open source infrastructure.

Mobile applications are another important category, less fully developed than some of the others mentioned here. All of the major mobile handset vendors are including Linux-based devices in their product lines, creating an opportunity for downloadable applications, including games, that will run on those devices. The business possibilities seem most promising for those applications that take advantage of the unique properties of mobile devices, including location-based services, motion sensing and mobile social networking based on proximity.

Of course, the above suggestions are just a starting point, and some of them may turn out not to be so attractive over time, particularly as more people build open source applications and commercialize them. As with any other business concept, entrepreneurs must consider the market opportunity, including size and competition, as key steps in their initial analysis.

In conclusion, this collection of ideas for building a business on open source software ranges from those that can be undertaken by a single individual to those that may need a substantial organization with a significant financial investment. There are, undoubtedly, many other concepts that can and will be explored.

ACKNOWLEDGMENTS

The author gratefully acknowledges the valuable comments of Bob Bickel and Dirk Riehle on an earlier version of this work.

REFERENCES

Fink, M. (2003), *The Business and Economics of Linux and Open Source*, Englewood Cliffs, NJ: Prentice-Hall.

Goldman, R. and R. Gabriel (2005), *Innovation Happens Elsewhere*, San Francisco, CA: Morgan Kauffman.

Krishnamurthy, S. (2005), 'An analysis of open source business models', in J. Feller, B. Fitzgerald, S.A. Hissam and K.R. Lakhani (eds), *Perspectives on Free and Open Source Software*, Cambridge, MA: MIT Press, pp. 279–96.

Perens, B. (1998), 'The open source definition', reprinted in C. DiBona, S. Ockman and M. Stone (eds) (1999), *Open Sources: Voices from the Open Source Revolution*, Sebastopol, CA: O'Reilly, accessed May 2008 at www.oreilly.com/catalog/opensources/book/perens.html.

Riehle, D. (2007), 'The economic motivation of open source software: stakeholder perspectives', *IEEE Computer*, **40** (4), 25–32, accessed May 2008 at www.riehle.org/computer-science/research/2007/computer-2007-article.html.

Weber, S. (2004), *The Success of Open Source*, Cambridge, MA: Harvard University Press.

7. Using innovation, research and finance to build a company with a multi-option strategy

Roberto Siagri, Andrea Barbaro and Nicola Buttolo

BUSINESS IS A RISKY BUSINESS

Giving birth to a firm is a hard enterprise. Transforming an idea into a business is a risky job.

As Arie de Geus points out in his book *The Living Company* (1997), if we take a look at a firm's average life expectancy we find that it is around 12.5 years, regardless of its geographical location.[1] If we focus on multinational corporations, the average life expectancy goes up to about 45 years: this can give us an idea of how a company's life can be extended by expanding the company itself outside the national borders; as we would say today, by globalizing it.

Furthermore, Christensen and Raynor (2003) remind us that 75 per cent of new products launched by existing firms, including the best established, does not succeed on the market; with reference to investments, 80 per cent of the ones made by venture capitalists give no return; and if we look at how many firms are able to sustain an above-average growth rate for more than a few years, we count just one out of ten.

The challenge is then to find a development model able to create growth and sustain the company in the medium and long term. There is no need for companies to grow to be big come hell or high water, but there is the need to create a sort of ecosystem able to sustain both small and big companies, an ecosystem in which small companies striving to grow can easily do so.

Everywhere, company birth and development always take place in a harsh environment: 'Just like Dante, midway upon the journey of their life, men and organizations find themselves within a dark forest. The forest is the complexity of the reality that surrounds them' (De Toni and Comello, 2005). On the other side, the complexity of the environment represents precisely a source of opportunities: nobody knows in advance the territory of

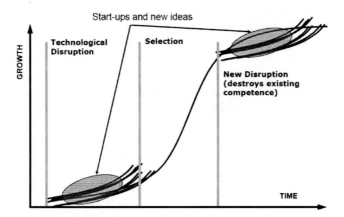

Figure 7.1   'S' curve (logistic curve, or sigmoid) applied to company development.

the future and nobody has yet the map of it: the future has to be imagined, even invented if needed, and we are the ones who will outline the map. As George Bernard Shaw once said: 'The people who get on in this world are the people who get up and look for the circumstances they want, and, if they can't find them, make them.'

TECHNOLOGICAL WAVES IN HIGH-TECH INDUSTRIES: SURFING BASICS

If we look at life cycles of products and technologies we can see that, from an evolutionary point of view, products and technologies are like human beings: they struggle to grow at the beginning of their existence, then grow very fast, after which they reach a plateau and in the end inexorably decline. It is therefore necessary to renew both products and their underlying technologies periodically. And this is indeed the purpose of continuous innovation.

Figure 7.1 shows a curve called 'logistic curve' or 'sigmoid', or even just 'S' curve. It represents the development of biological organisms and it represents adequately also the development of companies.

During the initial stage you can see several interrupted curves: this is the so-called 'infantile mortality', which is very high for firms and is related to the ideas selection phase. Firms that are able to go over the first stage of development then deal with an exponential growth; but this phase also, at a certain point, comes to an end when firms reach maturity.

At this point, in order not to go toward decline, firms have to start again to innovate as they did in their start-up phase; and they have to keep in mind that ideas selection will still be strong and, again, only the best ideas will survive.

Therefore, it is appropriate for firms to build up a portfolio of innovations in order to maximize the probability to be able at any time to restart with a new 'S' curve, avoiding in this way decline and so death: unlike humans, in fact, firms can defeat death and perpetuate themselves.

In order to do that, it is necessary to put in place an ongoing innovation process, independent from the current position of the company on the 'S' curve, a position that is difficult to identify.

The paradox is that while the human life cycle is known – since we know how long is the growth period, when a human being becomes adult and then old – we know very little about our products and the technologies we adopt.

The challenge is just this: to be able to evaluate what point of the curve we are on. Nobody can positively tell us, because if it were a known fact then everybody could create a successful company. But it is precisely this uncertainty that hides big opportunities.

In this scenario small firms seem to have the most advantage to catch new opportunities, because they are endowed with great flexibility: this is why acquisitions made by big firms of small or medium enterprises can help big firms find new flexibility.

What we all know is that companies lose flexibility when they grow big. A way to recover flexibility without putting in place huge internal convulsions is to acquire other companies that can bring flexibility elements into the organization; companies that could even become the main body of the same organization in the future.

But there is also another way to blend stability with flexibility. There are also companies already (or still) flexible enough to surf a new technological wave: since it is very difficult for a given organization to surf two different waves simultaneously, the risk for these companies is then to lose too soon the revenues coming from the original business and hence not to be able to sustain the exploration of a new 'S' curve. The paradox is that the more a company is able to jump on a new curve, the more it risks to disrupt itself. The threat for already flexible companies, then, is to be destroyed by the lack of a 'stable' source of revenues and cash flow during the start-up phase of the 'new deal'. In this case an acquisition can still be the solution, but the criteria to choose the candidate companies to acquire is the opposite: this time the target is to find a stable company with good results on the present business (and no plans to change!) and then delegate to the acquired company the role of generating the revenues and cash flow to sustain the flexible company on its shift to a new business. This time the two companies could also have a similar size, but the overall approach is still the same: finding a good balance without putting in place huge internal changes by taking the best from different organizations.

EUROTECH GROUP: A STORY OF INNOVATION AND ACCELERATED GROWTH

Eurotech was born in 1992, when a group of young technicians founded it, based on the idea of miniaturizing the PC and using it in as yet unexplored applications. An 'ideas factory' model, open to Europe – and to the world – (Euro) and to new technologies (tech).

Today, Eurotech is a 'pocket multinational' active on a global scale, based in Italy and with operating locations in Europe, North America and Asia. It is a group active in the research, development and marketing of miniaturized computers (NanoPCs) and in the field of high-performance computers (HPC).

Even before creating Eurotech, its founders were clear that – to compete successfully in an effervescent market such as the one of embedded computers in the 1990s – it was vitally important to manage to emerge. To be able to embark on a growth course, Eurotech had to get out of the scrum very fast indeed. And it had to do so without needing a huge initial capital. This was why, right from the start, focusing on excellence seemed to be the key to standing out from the crowd, disposing of great intellectual capital but of little economic capital.

For Eurotech, this term – excellence – meant a combination of innovation and quality. But that combination as such was not enough. What was needed was an even more distinctive connotation of excellence, one that, above all, worked as well as possible in order to achieve sound growth. Because of this, it was immediately clear to everyone that excellence had to be sought within sector standards.

Given this, instead of investing in proprietary or totally customized solutions, Eurotech immediately believed in the standards' strength as a launch pad to project the entire company into the future. The founders had understood from the very outset that it was not enough to give customers high-performance products. Those products also had to be open to future evolutions of technology – which looks set to be overwhelming – whilst also saving on previous investments. Standards could therefore permit innovation based on continuity, endowing products with the prospect of relative compatibility with future discoveries without having to start each time from scratch. Although retaining the ability and skills to develop customized solutions for special uses or customers, Eurotech chose right from the start to seek excellence with solutions representing the state of the art of the most universally recognized standards.

The second important choice immediately made – and one which has turned out to be a winning one – was to be an 'ideas factory' without a 'machinery factory'. This is an approach called 'fabless'. Within the value chain Eurotech decided to perform research, development, engineering and prototyping, quality control and logistics. Production was outsourced to contract manufacturers in order not to invest in costly manufacturing equipment.

In today's world, in which atom (that is, matter) supremacy has been replaced by information supremacy, it is easier for companies to emerge: it is not necessary anymore to own production means, since they can be found through outsourcing; the important thing is to own ideas; capital can come later. While at the beginning of the twentieth century it was almost impossible to start a business without capital, today it is possible to build up a company with a very limited investment, at least at the beginning, and use external capital only later on.

This is also the story of Eurotech, which in fact was born in 1992 with just 50 million lire (about 25 000 euros) of capital. The beginning was slow, but characterized by a continuously accelerating growth; in 2001, after eight and a half years, the incubation phase came to an end and Eurotech entered into a new phase, supported by private equity funding; in 2005, after only four and a half years, the private equity phase was concluded, since Eurotech S.p.A., the parent company of the Eurotech Group, was listed in the Star segment of the Milan Stock Exchange.

In 2002, ten years after its establishment, Eurotech started to make acquisitions, which after the IPO have become closer to each other on a time basis and also bigger in terms of dimension of the acquired companies.

But what is the rationale behind this growth acceleration through external means?

In Eurotech we quickly initiated an external growth strategy with the aim of achieving a critical mass (or 'tipping point') on a fast-track basis. To grow fast, we had to achieve equally fast entry of markets that for us were new, like France, the UK or USA. Starting from scratch, without a customer base and without a brand reputation, increased risks and the time needed. This is why we have used the acquisition lever: we wanted to grow at a rate of 50 per cent year-over-year and to maintain that pace we needed acceleration factors that could be found only by going beyond the original company's boundaries. Good ideas (we can call them 'potential innovations') are good to start, but often not enough to grow fast.

Acquisitions were evaluated according to the geographical location of the firms, or according to their customer base or their network of relationships. We also looked for companies close to the maturity stage of their first 'S' curve, that is, companies ready to start climbing a second curve, but for some reason not yet doing so: in other words, industrially and financially sound companies with unexpressed growth potential.

In the period from 2002 to 2007 we made significant acquisitions and achieved a compound annual growth rate (CAGR) of 55.9 per cent.

Through acquisitions of foreign companies we have also tried to leave behind the 'country effect', that is, on the one side, the dependence of the company on the course of a given national economy or a given currency and, on the other side, the presence of cultural barriers to entry into foreign markets.

An aspect we would like to highlight here is the attitude each company should have towards globalization. According to the famous science fiction writer William Gibson, 'the future has already arrived. It's just not evenly distributed yet.' This means that what we call 'future' could be already happening somewhere in the world: the key point is then to be there to meet it.

Being global today is no more a choice but a necessity: it is more important to be global than to be big. Here is where we go back to the fact that company size comes second: in a world that is more and more flat, as Friedman (2005) states in his book, *The World is Flat*, big firms have to behave like the small ones and small ones like the big ones.

To summarize, the drivers for company growth and value increase are twofold: on one side there is the lever of innovation whilst, on the other side, there is the lever of mergers and acquisitions (M&A); and you have to use both. In fact, a company must face two problems: first, balancing with other sources of revenues the lack of returns from innovations during their incubation period; second, having a reference market big enough to allow a leadership position and to keep competitors away.

The underlying idea is that the enlargement of both the geographical base and the customer base should guarantee a better market introduction of innovative products. The target is then to trigger a virtuous circle able to feed itself: company size sustains innovation, innovation sustains growth, and the result of growth is again a greater company size.

FOLLOWING THE TRAIL OF FUTURE INNOVATIONS: THE ROLE OF MINORITY INTERESTS

Eurotech does not only make acquisitions aimed at taking full control of the acquired company and in this way at increasing the Group's consolidated revenues. Eurotech invests also in minority interests in start-ups working on technologies and market segments with a high potential, which help to explore future opportunities. You can see them as small financial operations someway in between business angels and venture capitals; Eurotech considers these minority interests as 'real options' on innovations and future markets.

A real option represents a right – not an obligation – to take an action on an underlying non-financial asset, referred to as a real asset. The action may involve abandoning, expanding or contracting a project or even deferring the decision until a later time (Kodukula and Papudesu, 2006).

When projects are highly time-interdependent, making strategy is managing the firm's portfolio of real options. Any investment project whose implementation can be deferred, modified or which creates new investment opportunities can be analysed using this framework, called a real options approach (ROA).

Traditional valuation metrics, as net present value (NPV) or discounted cash flow (DCF), have the following deficiency: they ignore or cannot properly capture management's ability to review its original operating strategy if and when, as uncertainty is resolved, future events turn out differently from what management expected as the outcome.

In order to estimate the financial flows generated by a project you should determine *ex ante* the nature and the sequence of future decisions regarding the project itself. In reality, when measuring the value of a project, you have to notice that financial flows can be affected by some kinds of variability in comparison to what was estimated. This gap can derive from having put into effect decisions that are different from the assumed ones (internal uncertainty); or from having achieved results not corresponding to the estimated ones, even with an implemented plan fully compliant with the original one (external uncertainty) (Bozzolan, 2001).

Unlike other approaches, the options based technique of contingent claims analysis (CCA) explicitly recognizes that management's flexibility in adapting its future actions, contingent on future events, introduces an 'asymmetry' or 'skewedness' in the distribution of the project's value. This asymmetry results in an expansion of the investment opportunity's value *vis-à-vis* standard NPV analysis because future management decisions can improve upside potential while at the same time limiting downside losses. This asymmetry introduced by managerial flexibility calls for an expanded NPV criterion that reflects both sources of a project's value, the traditional static NPV of directly measurable cash flows, and a premium for the flexibility embedded in its operating options. That is, Expanded (strategic) NPV = Static (passive) NPV of expected cash flows + Option premium (active management).

By going beyond the limit of traditional methodologies, the ROA attempts to evaluate investment projects characterized by high uncertainty through the assumption that managerial flexibility is a necessary tool for the company's value creation.

The ROA is made by three consecutive steps: real options analysis, aiming at the identification of options in the considered investment project; real options valuation (ROV), consisting of building the cash flow model and in shaping the uncertainty, in order to be able to evaluate the value of the options; and real options management (ROM), through which options are managed (management of the expiration date, of the uncertainty left and of the option and strike price). This whole system is also called the real options management system.

Such an approach puts uncertainty under a new perspective, transforming it into a source of potential value. In fact, ROV derives from its capability to make the investment's payoff curve asymmetric, thus preserving the company from negative situations and events, while allowing it to take advantage of positive evolutions of the business.

The main source of value for an investment is no longer represented by the expected cash flows, but rather by future expansion opportunities that each project has, namely by the real options built in it.

From this perspective, real options are an answer to the need of managing uncertainty. Through this mechanism, the M&A lever can grant potential for rapid change and allow companies to be prepared to surf future technological waves. That is why all big high-tech corporations (IBM, Microsoft, Google and so on) make acquisitions not sporadically but on a monthly basis. The point is that there is no confidence that a big firm can manage to stay big forever and nobody knows what the future will be like.

In order to identify the right innovative companies to invest in, it is important then to understand very well which are the trends that will shape the future; and, as Sony's founder Akio Morita used to say, you have to look ten years ahead.

TRUE INNOVATION COULD DESTROY YOUR COMPANY: SO, HOW DO YOU HANDLE IT?

Let us go back to the innovation issue. If you analyse the topic deeply enough you realize that, to tell the truth, everybody talks about innovation, but only a few are really ready for it. This is because innovation is, in a certain way, not natural for established companies, since their main intention is usually to preserve their status, while true innovation tends to break the status quo.

In the analysis about company development that Christensen makes in his book, *The Innovator's Dilemma* (1997), the author brings back the problems of growing and surviving in the medium to long term to the difficulties of innovating. And in his subsequent book, *The Innovator's Solution*, he highlights that 'Innovation fails because organizations unwittingly strip the disruptive potential from new ideas before they ever see the light of day' (Christensen and Raynor, 2003 front flap of jacket).

Innovation is then not only a technological matter or a financial matter: according to Christensen and also to our experience, innovation is, in the end, a matter of humans and culture, because true innovation is disruptive and disruptive innovation requires a will to change.

In order to better understand what disruptive innovation is it could be useful to remember what Morita, the founder of Sony, used to say: 'If you ask the public what they think they will need, you will always be behind in this world. You will never catch up unless you think one to ten years in advance and create a market for the items you think the public will accept at that time' (minidisk.org, 2008).

So, in order to truly innovate, you have to have a person or a small team that thinks ahead; you need a small portion of the organization constantly projected into the future.

But how can a company handle disruptive innovation without destroying itself? The innovation model used by Eurotech in order to prevent the decline and start a continuous innovation process is inspired by the ideas of Clayton Christensen. According to his vision, there are two types of technologies: sustaining and disruptive.

In Figure 7.2 there are two inclined arrows representing the growth path of the two different technologies, while the two grey stripes indicate the customers/market absorption capacity of these two technologies.

One key concept expressed by Figure 7.2 is that the market is not able to absorb innovations at any pace: the market is like each one of us, so when it gets used to a certain technology it cannot switch immediately to a new one; in other words, the market does not accept changes too fast.

Another key concept shown in Figure 7.2 is that there are two limits on market absorption capacity: a lower one, easy to understand and strictly linked with minimum accepted product performance, but also an upper one that is more difficult to grasp. In fact, some companies make the mistake of innovating too much and too long in the same direction, until they reach a product performance that is no longer accepted by the market, either because it is too expensive or because it is too complex. In other words, the market does not need that much.

Here's why innovation is not the medication for all diseases: even being too innovative on sustaining technologies can be dangerous, since it can

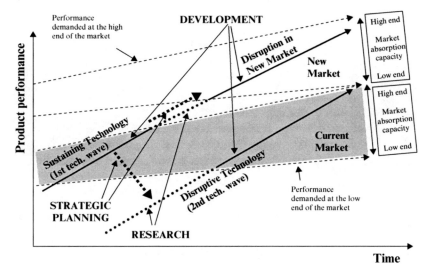

Figure 7.2   Eurotech's innovation model.

bring products out of the demand range – unless you are able to find new markets, in which you can exploit the excess of product performance generated by the excess of potential of the sustaining technology.

The key is to understand when it is time to switch to a different technological curve; which is the right moment to enter in the market with a different technology, able to reduce products cost or even to completely change the way in which products are conceived.

There is no need for a company to always make disruptive innovations. In reality, periods of stability are much more common than periods of fast change. Stability periods are necessary too, because they are the ones in which you exploit the market potential of your innovative products. Anyway, you need to find an innovation model that allows the company to easily switch from stability to rapid change when needed.

But there is another hidden danger: you have to take into account short-term overestimates. Figure 7.3 shows the 'hype cycle', a graphic representation of the maturity and adoption of specific technologies over time. The term was coined by Gartner, an analyst/research house, based in the USA, that provides opinions, advice and data on the global information technology industry. Since 1995, Gartner has used hype cycles to characterize the overenthusiasm or 'hype' and subsequent disappointment that typically

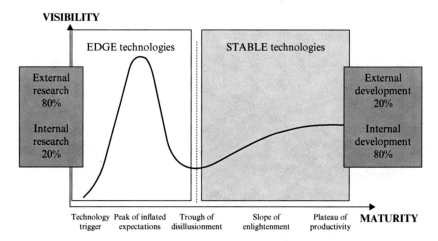

Figure 7.3   Technologies and the Gartner hype cycle.

happens with the introduction of new technologies. In other words, individuals tends to overestimate in the short term the success of a product/ technology and to underestimate the effects in the medium to long term. This type of behaviour is the same that gives birth to economic bubbles.

Hype cycles also show how and when technologies move beyond the hype, offer practical benefits and become widely accepted. According to Gartner, hype cycles aim to separate the hype from the reality, and enable CIOs and CEOs to decide whether or not a particular technology is ready for adoption.[2]

From the curve in Figure 7.3 you can also derive indications on how to set up a good way to allocate resources for research and development. Using the rule of the thumb (the 80/20 rule) and considering technologies before the 'trough of disillusionment' as technologies to be addressed with research and the other ones as technologies to be addressed with development, a 'design criteria' could be to externalize 80 per cent of research activities to universities and research centres and to keep the remaining 20 per cent for the internal resources; a dual approach could be used for development activities, that is, you could assign 80 per cent of them to the internal resources and externalize only the remaining 20 per cent.

From the 'design principles' or 'meta models' we have seen so far, you have then to pass to an operative organizational model built around and propelled by innovation. And when one talks of innovations, there are generally two types of approaches: technology push and market pull. The first approach starts from what technology is able to give, whilst the second starts from what the market demands or is able to absorb. They are two

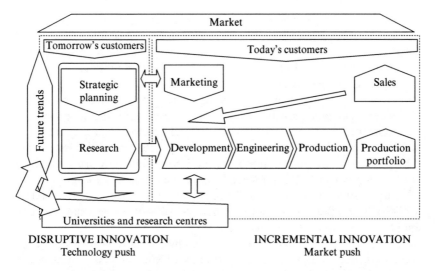

Figure 7.4   Eurotech's business model, propelled by innovation.

opposing approaches – but they can be effectively combined. And this is what we have chosen to do in Eurotech.

In fact, to effectively combine the two approaches, we have developed an organizational model in which we have segregated research from development: research works on the technological curve outside the market demand, whilst development takes care of the technological curve within the current demand (Figure 7.2).

Therefore, research and development follow the technological curve in completely different stages and hence require different people with different ways of thinking. Development (the origin of incremental innovation) is driven by customers and by marketing, in other words, by the market: it is market pull. Research (intended here as applied and directed to the study of products not yet requested by the market) is driven by technology development and by its effects on humans, and gives course to new products according to a technology-push approach (Figure 7.4).

For a company like ours, which very much bases its success on technological innovation and on anticipating demand, it is essential that research be driven by a technology-push approach. Only with this approach is it possible to maintain technological leadership and continue developing state-of-the-art solutions. To make the technology-push approach more effective and efficient, the network of outside relations with the 'knowledge network' is vitally important: this permits parallel exploration, at limited cost, of several alternative paths.

The centre of gravity of technology-push research is therefore very much skewed towards the outside world, with a target outside/inside ratio of 80:20. Given this, in order to maintain an effective hold over research, it is important that control be centralized at parent company level.

Since research works outside the demand curve, it is driven by company direction, that is, by strategic planning which, starting from the vision, defines the guidelines for future scenarios exploration. In this process, it is important for top managers to use foresight methods, based on critical thinking applied to depict possible alternative futures in the long term. These methods are quite common in the USA, while they are generally a lot less familiar in Italy. In a few words, the exercise of foresight aims to identify positive trends in 10 or 20 years from now. Alternative scenarios will be a major part of the output, while the decision about what future to build can also involve other mechanisms.

There is, however, intrinsic difficulty in understanding which will be the next driver technology or the next winning product. To do so, it is necessary to try, test and explore. It must also be said that this exploration of virgin paths might not even produce any result at all. Some paths may in fact turn out not to be feasible or, more simply, not economically viable. If the life cycle tells us that sooner or later our product will decline, the question is: among the many technological alternatives, not all of which are winners, which is the right one? Some technologies are doomed to die before they even get to market; others instead will enter the market and the market will determine its development. In order to maintain our technological leadership, we have to explore as many evolutionary scenarios as possible. To do so, combining efficacy and moderate costs, we use outside partnerships. Because of this, we have set up many relationships with universities and research centres – and in 2005 we also set up a scientific committee to manage this 'knowledge network'. And it is all based on two fundamentals, that is, sharing of the innovation model and sharing of evolutionary scenarios. It is a win-win relationship: the university does research on topics that will not remain in a drawer, because they are 'sponsored' by a company; and the company can lever a network of researchers with a capacity for parallel exploration of different scenarios that it would otherwise be impossible to create.

The development part is a different matter. In order to effectively launch research results on the market, it is important to focus on an approach that indeed starts from what the markets want or may appreciate. The right approach for development is market pull. Moreover, whilst research benefits from the simultaneous existence of several open fronts, development has to converge towards a product or product family – and it is therefore advisable to limit dispersion of energy and outside interference. Another peculiarity of development is that it necessarily features the entry into play of the specifics of sectors and geographical areas – and centralized control would not permit adequate understanding/ exploitation of such specifics. Because of this, development is decentralized and distributed among the various Group companies. By so doing, each of them can conjugate a given product idea in the best way, understand/exploit local specifics and turn research results into a commercial success.

So far so good; but there is another part of the story: since research and development start from different points of view and use different approaches, linking the former with the latter is a true organizational challenge. There is no doubt that the two processes need to stay separated, but it is also clear that there are points in time when innovation has to flow from research to development in order to reach the market and generate revenues. As a matter of fact, what are supposed to be 'points of contact' between research and development turn out to be 'points of collision'. Here's why it is so important for research to be driven by strategic planning, that is, by the top managers of the company: when collision happens, innovations ready for the market, but facing an excess of inertia on moving quickly to development, need good 'sponsors'. It is a matter of change management: the ability of top managers to lead the change required by innovation is paramount.

MULTI-OPTION STRATEGY: BUILDING A POISED ORGANIZATION

The only fixed elements of a company in the medium to long term are the vision, the mission and the values. The business model is instead an element that evolves continuously: in order to grow you often need to change, and for a company changing means in the end changing its own business model; and when a company wants to grow fast, then the business model might need to be changed swiftly too. Especially when dealing with high-tech industries, in fact, the ability to grow, exploiting a new product or technology, is often related to the development of a specific logic and a tailored system of activities to carry on the business in the new scenario.

The point is that companies have to be ambidextrous[3] and multitasking: while the right hand is taking care of the current product or technology, the left hand must be working on the next ones.

In fact, the first key element of a strategy based on a dynamic equilibrium driven by innovation is a high adaptability capacity (Figure 7.5).

Strategy based on dynamic equilibrium driven by innovation:

- High adaptability capacity
- Incremental innovation
- Disruptive innovation
- Knowledge network

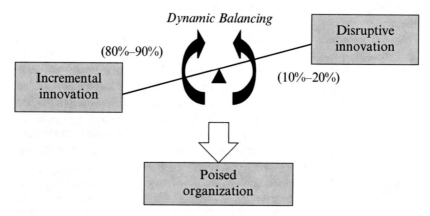

Source: Inspired by Davenport et al. (2006).

*Figure 7.5   Eurotech's multi-option strategy to build a poised
             organization.*

The second key element is the combination of sustaining and disruptive innovation: enterprises require both incremental and breakthrough
innovation capabilities to survive. In fact, incremental innovations are
fundamental in the short term, but are not sufficient to sustain growth and
perpetuity; on the other hand, disruptive ideas, if not well managed, burn
out cash, even if they might generate tremendous future cash flow.

The third key element is the knowledge network: in today's economy
innovation for new value creation arises from collaboration in networks
which include business ecosystems, traditional industry clusters and supply
and demand chains, but also universities, research institutes, consortiums,
associations and so on. Astute leveraging of knowledge networks for value
innovation, with relevant internal company functions moving outside the
enterprise, is becoming a key success factor for enterprises.

All these key elements are necessary to build up what we have called a
'multi-option strategy': the overall term distinguishes our approach from
strategy as planning, balancing, positioning (fit) and resource leveraging
– the traditional approaches. It is based on managing several new

business models simultaneously. Managing only one business model that usually becomes quickly 'traditional', with future continued success not guaranteed, is inadequate in the innovation economy: enterprises require a portfolio of new business models, ready to replace the established one.

A significant portion of these new business models can also exist in other small organizations, partially owned by the current one through minority interests: here's another reason why the acquisition of minority interests is as strategically important as the acquisitions aimed to increase the overall size of the company.

And partnering with big companies is a good choice for small companies too. Thompson (2006), for example, emphasizes that is definitely a win-win approach: small companies who partner with larger companies have much to gain, so not only big companies should look for 'real option' relationships (Raynor, 2007), but also smaller companies who want to grow should seek for alliances with the big brothers.

The application of this multi-option strategy both implies and requires the creation of a 'poised organization'. The concept 'organizational poise' refers to a dynamic capability rooted in a specific mindset, a range of diverse 'ambidextrous' capabilities, and an ability to effectively rejuvenate itself. An 'unpoised' organization may suffer from limitations in managerial mindsets, narrow range of dexterities and/or paralysing inertia (Davenport, Leibold and Voelpel, 2006).

The poised organization is the place in which incremental and disruptive innovation cohabit, but also the result of the simultaneous use of the two types of innovation. In fact, it the beginning the poised organization is the incubator of the disruptive innovation, but after the first disruption the poised organization itself is shaped by the new course of action. The role of research is to be the fuel for disruptive innovation, while the role of development is to be the fuel for incremental innovation. In this organizational environment the M&A lever has a dual role: it provides a greater company size, to both exploit and sustain innovation, but also brings flexibility elements into the organization, to keep it open to new high-potential trends and agile enough to last and perpetuate itself.

Poised organizations 'genetically' have the ability to deal with uncertainty, because they are intrinsically used to live without fixed reference models and to fluctuate between opposite positions.

This ability is very important and must be preserved, because uncertainty is, in the end, the true source of great opportunities.

As we have underlined at the beginning, nobody knows in advance the territory of the future and nobody has yet the map of it. So there is no reason why you have to wait to walk your way if you feel it is the right one: you can track the path to success only after you go through it.

NOTES

1. The author quotes a Dutch survey of corporate life expectancy in Japan and Europe.
2. http://en.wikipedia.org/wiki/Hype_cycle.
3. For a thesis about ambidextrous organizations, see Tushman and O'Reilly (1997).

BIBLIOGRAPHY

Bozzolan, Saverio (2001), *Bilancio e Valore: metodi e tecniche di simuiazione*, Milan: McGraw Hill Italia.
Christensen, Clayton M. (1997), *The Innovator's Dilemma. When New Technologies Cause Great Firms to Fail*, Boston, MA: HBS Publishing.
Christensen, Clayton M. and Michael E. Raynor (2003), *The Innovator's Solution. Creating and Sustaining Successful Growth*, Boston, MA: HBS Publishing.
Davenport, Thomas H., Marius Leibold, Sven C. Voelpel (2006), *Strategic Management in the Innovation Economy. Strategic Approaches and Tools for Dynamic Innovation Capabilities*, Erlangen, Germany: Publicis Publishing.
de Geus, Arie (1997), *The Living Company. Habits for Survival in a Turbulent Business Environment*, Boston, MA: Harvard Business School Press.
De Toni, Alberto F. and Luca Comello (2005), *Prede o Ragni. Uomini e Organizzazioni Nella Ragnatela della Complessità*, Torino: UTET.
Friedman, Thomas L. (2005), *The World is Flat. A Brief History of the Twenty-first Century*, New York: Farrar, Straus and Giroux.
Kester, W. Carl (1984), 'Today's options for tomorrow's growth', *Harvard Business Review*, **62** (2), 153–60.
Kodukula, Prasad and Chandra Papudesu (2006), *Project Valuation Using Real Options. A Practitioner's Guide*, Fort Lauderdale, FL: J. Ross Publishing.
Marzo, Giuseppe (2003a), 'Alle radici del valore. L'approccio delle opzioni reali (parte I)', *Tpoint*, **3**, 22–6.
Marzo, Giuseppe (2003b), 'Alle radici del valore. Come valutare le opzioni reali (parte II)', *Tpoint*, 4, 22–7.
Marzo, Giuseppe (2005), *Management, Valutazioni, Incertezza. Un'analisi Critica della Teoria delle Opzioni Reali*, Padova: CEDAM.
Myers, Stewart (1984), 'Finance theory and financial strategy', *Interfaces*, **14** (1), 126–7.
Raynor, Michael E. (2007), *The Strategy Paradox. Why Committing to Success Leads to Failure (and What To Do About It)*, New York: Doubleday.
Thomson, David G. (2006), *Blueprint to a Billion. 7 Essentials to Achieve Exponential Growth*, Hoboken, NJ: John Wiley & Sons.
Trigeorgis, Lenos (ed.) (1995), *Real Options in Capital Investment. Models, Strategies, and Applications*, Westport, CT: Praeger.
Trigeorgis, Lenos and Scott P. Mason (1987), 'Valuing managerial flexibility', *Midland Corporate Finance Journal*, **5** (1), 14–21.
Tushman, Michael L. and Charles A. O'Reilly (1997), *Winning Through Innovation. A Practical Guide to Leading Organizational Change and Renewal*, Boston, MA: Harvard Business School Publishing.
Ventriglia, Francescopaolo (2005), *Strategie di Innovazione. Opzioni e Problematiche Valutative*, Turin, Italy: Giappichelli.

Other Sources

Eurotech Group (2007), *Annual Report 2007*, Udine, Italy.
Siagri, Roberto and Nicola Buttolo (2007), 'Creare, misurare e valorizzare l'innovazione. Il caso Eurotech', presentation given at Innovaction 2007.
http://en.wikipedia.org/wiki/Hype_cycle, accessed 23 April, 2008.
http://en.wikipedia.org/wiki/Foresight_%28futures_studies%29, accessed 23 April, 2008.
http://www.minidisc.org/econ113-paper.htm, accessed 10 November, 2008.

8. Technology entrepreneurship education: the Intel–UC Berkeley Global Entrepreneurship Education Initiative

Mark Harris

INTRODUCTION

At Intel and at UC Berkeley we believe that economic growth can be fueled by innovation. We also believe that innovation may be fostered through educational processes. So innovation fueled economic growth starts with education.

We see the greatest immediate leverage at the borderline between academia and industry. Many times after presenting the Intel–UC Berkeley Global Entrepreneurial Education Initiative we have been asked about our motivation to engage in this area and at this level. So in the following I would like to start by giving you some puzzle pieces of our motivation to create this program. The puzzle pieces should give you the bigger picture. Thereafter I will give you an overview of the program.

We have seen a number of issues hindering innovation and economic growth:

- Dramatic sustained drop (40–60 per cent) of student interest in science related disciplines and a resulting drop in innovation potential.
- Shortfall in IT specialists. At the same time an enormous increase in demand for information technology specialists with more than 1.6 million open IT jobs that cannot be filled by European Union (EU) citizens by the end of 2008, composed of a shortfall of 615 000 technicians and engineers (Reding, 2006) and almost 1 million new jobs created as a consequence of combined Western (+6.1 per cent) and Eastern (+13.2 per cent) European IT market growth (Accenture, 2005).
- Youth unemployment. Moving to unemployment in the EU we have a very diverse picture. In Denmark we are close to 3 per cent

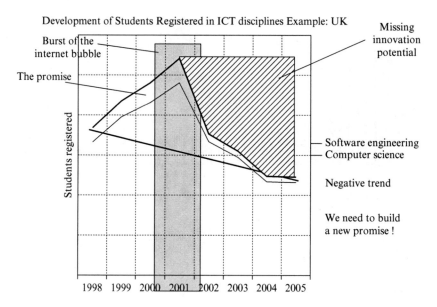

Source: University of Newcastle, UK.

Figure 8.1   Decline in interest for ICT disciplines in universities (back to pre-1997 levels).

unemployment, which is basically considered as full employment, compared with more than 10 per cent in Slovakia. In the USA it is at 4.6 per cent and in the EU 27 at about 6.8 per cent (Eurostat, 2007a). What is of real concern is the almost unanimously high unemployment rates of those aged 25 and under, which can reach almost 25 per cent (Figure 8.2).

This generation is our future and we need to put focus programs in place to help drive these numbers downwards. We believe strongly that innovation fueled economic growth is the way to create new high-tech jobs, and in the follow-on additional service positions.

- Poverty. Unfortunately data for poverty rates are not as consistent and easily available as unemployment rates but here also we see some major areas of concern. Within the EU we have some poverty rates similar to Third World countries. Also of concern is that this is not only in the emerging markets of the EU, such as Romania, Slovakia, Poland or Bulgaria, but also in countries like Spain and the UK. Really no level of poverty is acceptable, but it seems that economically very healthy countries are also at around 5 per cent.

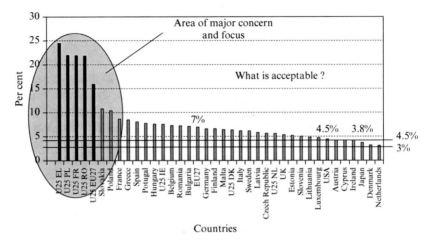

Source: Eurostat (2007b).

Figure 8.2   Unemployment in the EU.

● Brain drain. Brain drain is a result of not having appropriate
   opportunities within the country. Most people would prefer to
   stay close to their culture and country if they had comparable
   opportunities. Some of the numbers here are not surprising, but if
   we look at the countries in shaded bars in Figure 8.3, these are EU
   countries, with Italy, Hungary, Poland, Greece, France, Estonia
   and the Czech Republic all between 40 and 50 per cent brain drain
   (World Economic Forum, 2004). These are lost resources to the
   economy. If they return after a few years of course they can enrich
   the economy (brain exchange), bringing back expertise and a
   network, but how can they return if there is still no opportunity in
   their country.
   A model needs to be built, now, so that these resources leaving
   these countries will have the opportunity to come back at some point
   in time in the future, and in order to reduce the numbers of people
   who choose to leave the country in pursuit of opportunity. So what
   is appropriate? What is acceptable? If we draw a line where we have
   countries that import resources as well as export resources, this
   'balance' is a level probably acceptable to an economy. Looking at
   the data available, this seems to be at about 25 per cent. We need to
   drive those countries that have 40–50 per cent brain drain down to
   about 25 per cent, which again means we need to create an ecosystem
   that can create local opportunities for those individuals.

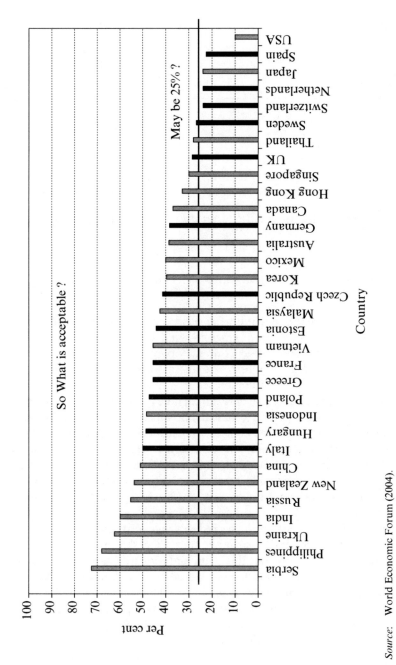

Source: World Economic Forum (2004).

Figure 8.3   Brain drain in the EU.

143

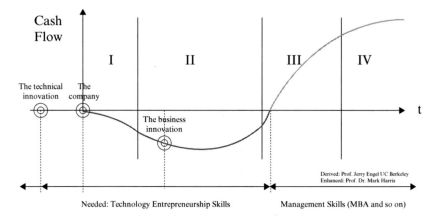

So Technology Entrepreneurship is not only 'What', but also 'When' !!

Source: Adapted from J. Engel, University of UC Berkeley.

Figure 8.4   What is technological entrepreneurship?

The aforementioned issues raise the need for innovation fueled economic growth and prosperity in emerging and developing markets and it is where technology entrepreneurship may play a role. So what is technology entrepreneurship? Figure 8.4 represents our view of technology entrepreneurship.

We are looking at a scenario where initially the innovation is of a technical nature. One has an idea for a technical innovation and over time decides to create a company. With the company creation a formal measurement of cash flow starts, and typically this cash flow is negative, burning some of the initial funding in development and evaluation before bringing on additional talent and eventually reaching the business innovation: How do I take this product to market or to my customers? How do I reach the mass market?

Assuming all of these can be answered, revenue also starts flowing and at some point revenues exceed spending and the cash flow starts to turn around and become positive. At this point and forwards, traditional management skills are needed, skills that you would typically find with an MBA graduate. In the preceding phase, from the technical innovation all the way through to the point of positive cash flow, technology entrepreneurship skills are needed. This is the sweet spot for true technology entrepreneurs. So technology entrepreneurship is not only 'what' but also 'when'.

THE INTEL–UC BERKELEY GLOBAL ENTREPRENEURSHIP EDUCATION INITIATIVE

The Intel–UC Berkeley Global Entrepreneurship Education Initiative is a program focused on accelerating the rate of innovation and economic growth in key markets around the world, centered on the diffusion of entrepreneurship.

Students pursuing degrees in engineering are prime candidates to drive tomorrow's technology entrepreneurship. To encourage and prepare them, the Intel® Higher Education Program sponsors a curriculum in entrepreneurship education, which includes three interrelated programs (Figure 8.5) aimed, respectively, to:

- Train academic faculty about the concept and value of technology entrepreneurship, and demonstrate how to build programs that drive new uses of technology and promote its successful commercialization – the 'Technology Entrepreneurship Education Theory to Practice Seminars' in collaboration with the Lester Center for Entrepreneurship and Innovation at UC Berkeley. The program, organized as a series of seminars, is designed for engineering or

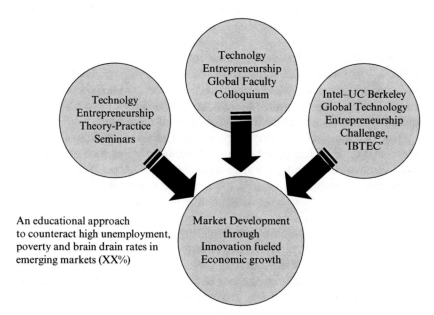

Figure 8.5   The Intel–UC Berkley Global Entrepreneurship Initiative.

science faculty at technology-oriented schools, and faculty from
complementary business programs.
- Demonstrate and share tools and methodologies that enable entrepreneurial training and development in higher education – the 'Global
Faculty Colloquium'. The program is designed as two weeks of training at UC Berkeley on rigorous details of entrepreneurship education,
ecosystem development and immersion into the Berkeley system.
- Practice entrepreneurship education, beyond traditional lab-based
technologies lecturing, through a full immersion in a business
plan competition – the 'Intel–UC Berkeley Global Technology
Entrepreneurship Challenge' – that is used as a real-life platform for
educational purposes.

The Technology Entrepreneurship Education Theory to Practice Seminars

These seminars will be taught by faculty from the Lester Center for
Entrepreneurship and Innovation at UC Berkeley's Haas School of Business,
which is recognized as a leader in entrepreneurship education and research.
'By providing the know-how to teach budding entrepreneurs how to commercialize new technologies and innovations, this program has the ability to
kick-start economic engines whose potential has lain dormant until now',
said Jerome Engel, executive director of the Lester Center, who will lead the
program. Engel has been teaching entrepreneurship and venture financing
at the Haas School of Business for 16 years. He served as faculty director
of the PriceBabson@Berkeley program and of the Kauffman Foundation's
Lifelong Learning for Entrepreneurship Educators program. The Haas–Intel
program will provide a framework and curriculum that college faculty can
adapt to their local situations, Engel said, 'building on a proven approach,
ultimately encouraging entrepreneurship around the world.'

'Not all countries have adopted entrepreneurship as a means of growing
their markets and creating jobs', said Christian Morales, vice president of
sales and marketing and general manager of Intel Europe. 'Today, by and
large, many educational systems are geared toward creating employees,
not entrepreneurs. To change this dynamic, the core curriculum at universities should add basic instruction in what it takes to start and operate a
company, including training in formulating a strategy, writing a business
plan, marketing, finance and raising capital.'

The program will offer a teaching curriculum, classroom exercises and
other tools for university professors to teach the basics of entrepreneurship to engineers and scientists, creating innovative business people with
cross-disciplinary skills, technical expertise and the ability to seize market
opportunities.

Faculty attending the program are encouraged to share with faculty at other schools how they apply their newly gained knowledge.

The Global Faculty Colloquium

The Global Faculty Colloquium is two weeks of training on rigorous details of entrepreneurship education, ecosystem development and immersion into the operations of the Berkeley entrepreneurship program. We will also make extensive use of the experiences and situations of the participants to drive localization of programs and best practices. At the end of the two-week session participants will leave with a deep understanding of how they can create value at their institutions and in their regions. They will be prepared to be 'master faculty' in their local regions, complete with materials and skills to train others in their communities about entrepreneurship education.

As a participant in the colloquium, faculties will have the opportunity to:

1. Develop a broader perspective on entrepreneurship, its role in economic development and their own role in making entrepreneurship successful in their regions.
2. Focus on their own personal skills and development as a master faculty.
3. Learn from and assist other master faculties in completely different settings from their own.

This Global Faculty Colloquium will help faculties to frame the issues they are facing in relation to their peers and will help them build a global network. We expect each of the participants to create forums, classes and educational opportunities for other faculty in their region. The colloquium is built around several themes:

* The use of competition and experimentation as tools in building entrepreneurial tendencies in students. By observing the UC Berkeley Business Plan Competition, the participants will experience our brand of competition and how it is organized. We will weave several aspects of the competition into the colloquium.
* Expert modules that look deeply into entrepreneurship as a subject, from marketing to organization to finance.
* A central project that each faculty participant will complete. This project is aimed at creating the necessary materials for each faculty to train others in their region.

- Team projects to build a community among the participants and a sense of joint completion of the colloquium.
- Several opportunities for participants to contribute material to the seminar.

The Intel–UC Berkeley Technology Entrepreneurship Challenge

To encourage creativity by putting the theories of entrepreneurship to practice, Intel and the University of California, Berkeley sponsor the innovative Technology Entrepreneurship Challenge. The Challenge seeks business plans that commercialize new and truly innovative technologies to create a positive impact on society. Business plans chosen to compete make integral use of novel technology, including:

- Semiconductors, manufacturing and hardware
- Mobile and wireless
- Digital home and consumer electronics
- Retail and consumer software
- Enterprise software and IT
- Energy and power generation
- Nanotechnology
- Life sciences and biotechnology.

Upon nomination for entry into the Challenge by participating schools or through partner competitions, teams submit their business plans for review by the Challenge judging committee that will use a number of criteria structured to select the business opportunity with the greatest impact through the deployment of new technology. Emphasis is placed on the deployment of emerging and innovative technology products and services which have a high likelihood of generating significant benefits for both investors and the broader industry ecosystem. The judging committee will not be biased toward plans that generate the highest financial return. Nevertheless a requirement for entry is that the proposed businesses can achieve a positive return within a team's proposed investment time frame. Judges will be notable venture capitalists and other industry and entrepreneurship experts.

The winner of the 2008 Technology Entrepreneurship Challenge received a $25 000 cash prize. All participants will also benefit from publicity for their business plans, introductions to potential investors and feedback from industry experts.

Business plan teams may only enter the Challenge through nomination by a partner school or competition. Partner schools and competitions are chosen by the organizers of the Challenge based upon their history and qualifications. Plans which have progressed to the final round of the business plan competition of a partner school may enter. Each partner school may nominate up to two business plans in any one year. Teams or team members that have received any form or amount of venture capital financing for their business plan may not participate in the Challenge. Teams with seed financing from non-venture capital sources totaling less than $250 000 may compete in the Challenge, providing that the amount and source of all capital arrangements are clearly identified in the team's entry materials for the Challenge.

REFERENCES

Accenture (2005), 'Jobs of the future', in alliance with the Lisbon Council.
Eurostat, (2007a), 'EuroIndicators', news release 132/2007, October.
Eurostat, (2007b), 'Unemployment in the EU', 3 July, European Commission, Luxembourg.
Reding V. (2006), 'The role of ICT in innovation and growth', speech at Forum de la Nouvelle Economie, Madrid, 8 May.
World Economic Forum (2004), Global Competitiveness Report 2004–2005, London: Palgrave Macmillan.

Index

adaptability 135
advertising model of open source
    software 114–15
Ahuja, G. 101
Allen, K. R. xiii, xiv
alliances *see* networks
Amazon.com 116
American Electronics Association 15
'angels' *see* business angels
Apache Foundation 109
Apple 28
aPress 112

Baines, S. 98
BAMS Angels Fund 75–7
Bangladesh, microfinance in 2
BasecampHQ 114
Becattini, Giacomo 11
Beffa, Jean-Louis 35
Belgium, business angels in 75–7
Benetton 12
Berkeley Software Distribution (BSD)
    116
Berkeley University *see* UC Berkeley
biotechnology 15–16
BitRock 115
brain circulation 4
brain drain 19, 142–3
breakthrough innovation 136
Brusco, Sebastiano 11, 12
Burgelman, R. A. xi
Burt, R. S. 85, 86, 102
Bush, Vannevar 26–7
business angels xvi, 8, 63, 64–5, 67–9
    case study of BAMS Angels Fund
        75–7
    future of 78–9
    management 77–8
    structure of funds
        compensating managers 73
        equal *versus* free investment
            amounts 72–3

    investment process and decision-
        making 70–72
    legal/fiscal structure 74–5
    member-led *versus* manager-led
        organizations 69–70
    relationship with angel networks
        74
business concept xiv–xv
business model xv, xviii
    New Economy business model 9
    using open source software 110–19
business/entrepreneurial opportunities
    xi, xiv–xv

capital
    social 83–7, 95–6
    venture capital 2, 7–8, 53, 60, 63–4,
        67
    see also business angels
Carpenter, Marie 7
Casson, M. xi
Chell, E. 98
China 19–20
Christensen, Clayton M. 122, 130
CollabNet 112
collaboration *see* networks
communitarian policies for R&D 29–32
compensation systems 6–7
competitiveness, technological districts
    45
Competitiveness Poles initiative 33,
    34, 37
consulting services, open source
    software and 117–18
contingency argument 98–101
contingent claims analysis (CCA) 128
co-operatives 12
corporations 64
    building a poised organization 135–7
    social capital 83–7, 95–6
    see also small and medium
        enterprises (SMEs)